MW00533094

ᴀBIBLICIST VIEW

of Law and Gospel

Lester L. Stephenson

Col. 2:9

"God has given Lester a special gift for understanding and communicating the Bible message. Whether he communicates through writing or teaching, the message of truth is clear. In this book, he has fleshed out important truths of God's word in a thorough, systematic, and yet practical fashion. The reader will be blessed through this writing and will come away with a better understanding of God's work through God's word."

—DAVID J. WHITCOMB

Teaching pastor at Community Baptist Church

"A Biblicist View of Law and Gospel treats a most controversial theological subject thoroughly and scripturally. It underscores the value of Old Testament Law as a gracious revealer of divine character and an expose of human depravity as prerequisite to the gospel. The work provides a helpful critique of the two extremes that have plagued Christendom—legalism and antinomianism."

—GERALD PRIEST, PH.D.

Former professor of historical theology,
Detroit Baptist Theological Seminary

A BIBLICIST VIEW

of Law and Gospel

Lester L. Stephenson

AMBASSADOR INTERNATIONAL
GREENVILLE, SOUTH CAROLINA & BELFAST, NORTHERN IRELAND

www.ambassador-international.com

A Biblicist View of Law and Gospel

© 2017 by Lester L. Stephenson

All rights reserved

ISBN: 978-1-62020-156-5
eISBN: 978-1-62020-667-6

Scripture quotations taken from the New American Standard Bible® (NASB), Copyright © 1960, 1962, 1963, 1968, 1971, 1972, 1973, 1975, 1977, 1995 by The Lockman Foundation. Used by permission. www.Lockman.org

Scripture marked KJV taken from The King James Version, The Authorized Version. Public domain.

Scripture marked ESV taken from The ESV® Bible (The Holy Bible, English Standard Version®). ESV® Permanent Text Edition® (2016). Copyright © 2001 by Crossway, a publishing ministry of Good News Publishers. The ESV® text has been reproduced in cooperation with and by permission of Good News Publishers. Unauthorized reproduction of this publication is prohibited. All rights reserved.

The Amplified Bible Copyright © 2015 by The Lockman Foundation, La Habra, CA 90631. All rights reserved.

The Darby Translation Bible. Public domain.

Cover Design & Typesetting by Hannah Nichols

Ebook Conversion by Anna Riebe Raats

AMBASSADOR INTERNATIONAL
Emerald House
411 University Ridge, Suite B14
Greenville, SC 29601, USA
www.ambassador-international.com

AMBASSADOR BOOKS
The Mount
2 Woodstock Link
Belfast, BT6 8DD, Northern Ireland, UK
www.ambassadormedia.co.uk

The colophon is a trademark of Ambassador

I want to thank my pastor, David Whitcomb, for pointing out improvements and several instances of sloppy prose. Dr. Gerald Priest read it thoroughly and made many suggestions that made this book better. Perhaps they were being courteous, but they both asked for a copy when it was finished. I appreciate it.

Mostly I want to draw attention to my wonderful wife, Debbie. She carries a heavy burden, not the least of which is putting up with me for four decades and counting. Debbie frequently expressed confidence this book would be published. She is a tremendous encouragement and inspiration. Without her forbearance, this book would have never existed. She is special!

CONTENTS

PREFACE

FOR MANY YEARS, I ACCEPTED the standard mantra, "Christians are under grace, not law," as the way to view the relationship between the Law and the Gospel. Even after earning a seminary degree, little changed. I just thought I had a more expansive, big picture view. As I look back, I realize I did not really understand all that I thought I knew on the subject. Sadly, I was not alone in my confusion. There seems to be a universal misunderstanding of the Law and the Old Testament among fundamental Christians. Some misinformed believers fail to understand and appreciate that when Christ fulfilled the Law, He did not do away with it. Sadly, some go so far as to discount the law and the rest of the Old Testament as unnecessary in an age of grace. Their disdain is dangerous for when Christ fulfilled the Law, He completely satisfied all its righteous demands on humanity. There is a new relationship to the law and a new standard of obedience.

When I heard a radio preacher cite Matthew 5:17 to illustrate the usefulness of the Old Testament for Christians, it took me out of my comfort zone. I began to study with a desire to understand Matthew 5:17-20. Preconceived notions began to crumble. Fourteen single-spaced pages later, I realized I still did not fully understand the issue.

I read all of the epistles identifying every passage that I thought even remotely related to the law and its applicability to Christians. Then I did a detailed study of each passage. Some proved not applicable, but the rest are in this book. My own position on this topic wavered numerous times during the study especially when I found passages that strongly and emphatically supported one position over another.

Because my purpose here is to be a biblicist, I compared all so-called "competing passages" and attempted to reconcile them.

I began to read scholarly tomes on law and grace. Some great men of God have written excellent works that were edifying and a true joy. Their benefit went far beyond this book; my Christian walk is stronger for having read their books.

There was one point of agreement by all scholars. It did not matter if they were reformed, dispensationalist, Lutheran, or what their position was on continuity or discontinuity; they all were of one mind that there was a problem. It was fascinating to see each theologian write nearly identical treatises describing the difficulty. Yet, each scholar had a different solution in which he was completely convinced was biblical truth.

I found that disturbing. There are at least five major schools of thought on Law and Gospel. Four of them have to be wrong—perhaps all five. And that does not include the many variations of each. There are untold numbers of books trying to reconcile the issue. These books take many different approaches that frequently conflict with each other. Thus, many of them also have to be wrong. That means that much of the time Christian leaders teach a major tenet of the Christian religion incorrectly. That is frightening and ought to humble every man who preaches and teaches the Bible. Add in all the other areas of doctrinal differences in Christendom and the amount of Bible knowledge taught without a sure reference of what is true, and you will wonder why men have not been driven to their knees.

In my navy career, I had the good fortune to live in twelve states. That means I also had the misfortune to visit a great many very bad churches. At times, church hunting was an ordeal—liberal theology despite the name out front, Bible translation views that elevated a translation to the level of the virgin birth and six-day Creation, radical views on the second coming, and woefully poor levels of Bible knowledge, both in pew and pulpit. I found churches who did not

believe it was scriptural to help the poor. A preacher taught the church
began when Christ called the disciples. I came across many who did
not believe in missions. Several more never preached from the Old
Testament. I stumbled across a Bible college that ignored all of the
Old Testament, most of the Gospels, and structured their curriculum
around Paul's Epistles.

I know of at least one missionary who went to the foreign field
with a personal theology that was soundly Baptist but not necessarily
sound orthodoxy. He was failing and considering leaving the ministry.
Fortunately, another missionary borrowed money to visit him for two
weeks and showed him his error. His system of theology let him down.

The degree of unorthodox Christianity masquerading as true faith
is appalling. Many systems of theology have no system at all. One of
the reviewers of this book who spent a career teaching in several very
good Bible colleges was baffled at my comments on bad churches. He
is no neophyte; he knew such things existed but was unaware of how
prevalent it was.

The purpose of this book is threefold. The principle purpose is to
teach believers the proper place for the Old Testament and the Law in
New Testament Christianity.

A second purpose is to show people the Bible is still the proper
source for our Christian faith. There is an alternative to studying dog-
matic systems of theology created by men to support a denominational
position, which is not the best way to learn the Bible.

The final purpose for this book, which will be readily evident on
the following pages, is to share my admiration of the Old Testament.
I'm convinced that far too little attention is given to the "law, the
writings, and the Prophets."

Every possible effort has been made to avoid theological systems
of men. So many times, preachers and Bible scholars have stated that

Dr. So-and-So is a great theologian, but be careful when reading his work on certain topics because his theology is a little off in that area.

I'm not against theological systems because without a system, it would be impossible to teach the Bible. My contention is the system ought to be what the Bible says. I also contend that when men apply sound hermeneutical principles to Bible study, without the filter of denominational and positional bias, they will always learn what the Bible says. If Scripture is unclear, then men are not obligated to theorize, but rather to accept that God chose not to reveal that point.

When research showed good men differ on a passage, I did a word-by-word exegesis to ascertain the meaning. Every point I've made, I found scriptural evidence to prove. Many times when rereading and proofing my words, I would add a note in red: "find scriptural proof." When the proof did not exist, I used the delete key.

The result is a biblicist view on the efficacy of the Mosaic Law and the Old Testament in the Church Age. As with anything written by a fallible man, there is likely to be an error or a weakness. I pray there is no heresy. Also, I'm convinced that as time passes, God will give me new light on some portion of Scripture that will cause me to return to this book and make improvements.

One thing I do know. I'll be able to teach this subject with confidence. However, I also know that I will have to be very careful how I structure my lessons since they will likely conflict with many preconceived notions held by Bible-believing church members. Most believers will be glad to learn what this book contains, but they will have to be brought carefully to the realization that some of what they have long believed and understood may need correction.

CHAPTER 1

A BIBLICIST VIEW

DOES THE LAW OF MOSES apply to Christians? The question generates fierce debate throughout Christendom and has done so since the Book of Acts. It caused church splits and was the impetus for the formation of some denominations. Even the disciples had difficulty understanding Christ's intentions concerning the Mosaic Law.

Today, there is a tremendous amount of confusion among God's people concerning the application of the law in Christian faith and practice. The reason is simple; the mass of Christianity has never fully grasped the relationship between Law and Gospel. Numerous conflicting and inconsistent views abound. Over time, theologians manufactured some general distinctions between parts of the law to obey and parts to reject. Sadly, these distinctions do not follow a clear orthodox set of principles. Instead, they often follow whatever appears practical or convenient. Modern Christians will swear allegiance to the Ten Commandments but do not subscribe to a kosher diet and would never consider the ceremonial rites and sacrifices. Yet all are in the Law. Christ fulfilled some of these commands, and they do not apply to Christianity. Yet, Christians must know these commands and how they relate to God's plan of the ages.

Attempts by contemporary Christians to apply the Law to their faith and practice are popular among groups with cultic tendencies, perhaps because it fits with a legalistic approach used to control their members. On the other hand, liberal theologians dismiss not only the law but also most of the Old Testament as little more than rules a tribal god used to control his followers.

As bad as liberal church theology is, that is not the real problem. Much more serious are fundamentalists who fail to appreciate fully the relationship between the Testaments. "Without paying attention to both Law and Gospel, no one can make any sense of Scripture. Knowing about both gives the Christian a correct understanding of the Bible."[1]

Some Christians read of the imperfection of the Levitical system in Hebrews and figure that means the Law of Moses and the Old Testament is "imperfect." They contend "the perfect Law of Christ" replaced it. They never consider that such thinking means they are saying the perfect God has created something imperfect. Nor do they reconcile their theology with Romans 7:12, "So then, the Law is holy, and the commandment is holy and righteous and good." Not to mention that Jesus said in Matthew 5:17–18, "Do not think that I came to abolish the Law or the Prophets; I did not come to abolish but to fulfill. For truly I say to you, until heaven and earth pass away, not the smallest letter or stroke shall pass from the Law until all is accomplished." "No stronger words could be employed to affirm the divine authority of every part of the Old Testament; for the Law and the prophets mean the entire Old Testament Scriptures."[2]

Some Christians argue the believer is under moral law but not ceremonial law. Others agree that Christians are under moral law but not the penalties. Another view is the moral law is valid as a way of life but not for salvation. Some declare we are under the Sermon on the Mount, but not under the law of Sinai. There is another curious view that Christians are under the commandments of God, but not under

---

1 Rick Ritchie, What is This Law and Gospel Thing? *Modern Reformation*, March/April 1993, 7-11.
2 William Caven, The Testimony of Christ to the Old Testament, in *The Fundamentals*, vol. 1 R. A. Torrey, ed. reprint 1996, (Grand Rapids, MI: Baker Books, 1917), 213.

the Law of Moses. Yet, in the context of Mark 7:9–10, Jesus declares "the words of Moses are also the words of God."[3]

These groups often place a lower value on the Old Testament and the Mosaic Law. They shun the Old Testament and dismiss the Law as irrelevant in the age of grace. A common refrain among believers is "I am under grace, not under law." The danger of that casual statement is that it can lead to confusion. Of course true believers are under grace, but that does not nullify the Old Testament or the purpose of the law. Not having to practice the ceremonies and sacrifices of the law expands to mean nothing in the law or Old Testament is valid for Christians. That is a gross over-simplification of law and grace and does not begin to explain the vital biblical relationship between both Testaments as well as between Law and Gospel.

Beginning with the second century Gnostics, writers across two millennia have raised myriad objections to the Old Testament. One scholar complains, "The Old Testament is the master problem of theology."[4] Others wonder if the Old Testament should have any authority in the Christian era. Often denominational differences have their roots in the extent of Old Testament influence in the development of theological systems. A recurring question in a number of theological circles is whether the God of the Old Testament is the same God revealed in Jesus Christ.[5] Another question is how to reconcile "the kingdom of God, which is found in both Testaments, with Christianity since it is viewed as a new beginning with a New Covenant?"[6] These

---

3 This paragraph summarizes a list of wrong and inadequate definitions of Law and Gospel found in Alva J. McClain, *Law and Grace*. 1954. Reprint, (Chicago: Moody Press, 1967), 41-42.

4 Emil G. Kraeling, *The Old Testament since the Reformation*. (New York: Harper, 1955), 8.

5 The position taken in this book, which the author believes is correct, the biblicist view is the God in both Testaments is one and the same. God the Father sent God the Son to fulfill the Law. In doing so, God has now made a full revelation of Himself through His Son. At Pentecost, God the Holy Spirit put God's Word in believers' hearts.

6 Walter C. Kaiser, Jr., *Toward Rediscovering the Old Testament*. Paperback edition, 1991. (Grand Rapids, MI: Zondervan Publishing House, 1987), 25.

difficult concepts have led some preachers and teachers to be quick to point out that Jesus, at His death, nailed the law to the cross, and thus declared much of the Old Testament invalid for Church Age believers. Sadly, this thinking permeates some Christian circles, and the Old Testament has become nothing more than a source of charming stories for children's Sunday school classes.

Far too many modern Christians are biblically ignorant concerning the Old Testament and its relationship to the New. Consequently, this leads to a murky understanding of the relationship between Law and Gospel. This ignorance leads to an abysmal lack of knowledge of the Jewish foundation for Christianity. "Most Christians seem oblivious to the fact that the early church was composed almost entirely of Jews and that it was therefore thoroughly Jewish in its worship and customs."[7] It makes one wonder what modern Christians think Jesus and the apostles were talking about when they so frequently said, "It is written." What did they think the Bereans were studying when they searched the Scriptures? Do they even realize the New Testament did not exist at this point?

The result is a profound misunderstanding of many Bible doctrines. For example, study of end times prophecy is popular with nearly every Christian group. Yet how can they fully understand the book of Revelation, whose theme is "Behold, He is coming with the clouds, and every eye will see Him, even those who pierced Him; and all the tribes of the earth will mourn over Him" (Rev. 1:7)? They will never grasp the full import of that prophetic verse if they do not know that it is a combined quote from two Old Testament prophets found in Daniel 7:13 and Zechariah 12:10.

This book will attempt to clarify the value of the Old Testament and the Law to true Christian religion as well as show how the Law and Gospel are, not only related but also completely and thoroughly intertwined. New Testament writers used hundreds of quotes and made

---

7 David R. Reagan, Does the Law of Moses Apply to Christians? *Word and Work.* March 1995, 69-75.

untold references and allusions to events in the Old Testament. Many New Testament passages prove the validity of the Old Testament and the Law and show there is true and genuine agreement between the Testaments. On occasions, Old Testament passages provide foundational knowledge to understand New Testament truths. Other times, New Testament writers add detail that provides the clarity necessary for understanding an Old Testament event. Thus, the proof of the usefulness of the Old Testament to the Christian life is readily obvious in the New Testament. Essentially both the "Law and Gospel are categories through which we understand Scripture."[8]

There is a book in the Counterpoints series titled *Five Views on Law and Gospel.* Five scholars wrote lengthy essays on the tenets of five different theological systems. They also wrote rebuttals of each of the other contributors. In that interesting volume, Walter C. Kaiser, Jr., in a response scolding one of the other contributors, said, "We will certainly be wide of the mark in urging the church to have nothing to do with that law! In fact, to break the least of those laws to teach others to do the same will earn those interpreters the dubious honor of being called the 'least in the kingdom of heaven' (Matt. 5:19)."[9]

It is a grave mistake to draw a line in the Scriptures between Malachi and Matthew.

THEOLOGICAL SYSTEMS OF MEN

Steven McAvoy wrote, "All systems of theology are human efforts to understand and consider the implications of the person and character and attributes of God."[10] He is absolutely right about theological systems being human efforts. Nearly everyone has a system of theology.

---

8 Rick Ritchie, 7-11.
9 Kaiser maintains that the weightier issues of the Law of Moses are binding on believers today. Walter C. Kaiser, Jr., response to *The Inauguration of the Law of Christ with the Gospel of Christ: A Dispensational View.* by Wayne Strickland in Gundry, Stanley N. ed. *Five Views of Law and the Gospel,* (Grand Rapids: Zondervan, 1996), 304.
10 Steven L. McAvoy, Can Truth Be Known? In Mal Couch, ed. *The Fundamentals for the Twenty-first Century.* (Grand Rapids, MI: Kregel Publications, 2000), 44.

It may be wrong, misleading, blasphemous, or soundly biblical. Anyone who interprets Scripture must have a system of theology.[11]

Many scholars produce worthwhile efforts to explain what they believe (and what they think the church ought to believe). Such a task is unbelievably complex because God's revelation to men revealed in the Bible is complex. An exhaustive accounting and explanation of everything important for men to know from the Holy Scriptures is too much for men. But, with varying degrees of success, they try anyway. And they should try. It is a duty of men to learn as much as possible about the Scriptures for they are God's revelation of Himself to men.

Theological and confessional issues always predominate. A scholar's system of theology determines which texts he considers important. Invariably, they write a stalwart defense of their position. Unfortunately, their position sometimes takes precedence over what the Bible says. Oh, they are not heretics, nor apostate, just wedded at all costs to their system of theology.

Many tend to cite only authors who agree with them. When they mention differing opinions, it is only to disagree and point out error. Often they use the English rendering of a passage to buttress their position without reference to the original languages. Nor do they always follow sound hermeneutical principles; forgetting or ignoring that context is king.

Reading a book to learn what the Bible says on a subject can be difficult because what the author has to say often gets in the way. When reading men's books, it is frightening to see how many times they leave out passages of Scripture in their writing that conflict with their "system." It is quite common for authors to "proof text" a theological point. They select verses, seemingly at random and often out of context, from throughout the Bible to support their position. They select a position, then find a verse to back it up. Wrenching a verse out of context

---

11 I'm grateful to Dr. Gerald Priest for this principle. He went on to say that without a system, men could never comment on Scripture. They would be limited to quoting Scripture only.

without regard to the sense of a passage subordinates Scripture to man. Finding a biblical reference chosen only to prove a point means they failed to follow the example of the Bereans and search out "whether those things were so." Sometimes it is not so.

Some theologians have a tendency to engage in abstract speculation. They make things up that are not in the Bible or force meanings from one Testament to the other. It is reminiscent of Paul's words to Timothy, "For some men, straying from these things, have turned aside to fruitless discussion, wanting to be teachers of the Law, even though they do not understand either what they are saying or the matters about which they make confident assertions" (1 Tim. 1:6–7).

Equally bad are theological systems that indiscriminately mix Law and Gospel—a problem since the first century. The Judaizers contended that Judaism was still the true religion and was permanently binding. Christianity was only an addition. His Epistles reveal Paul was in near constant conflict with this group. Their commitment to circumcision required keeping the whole law. "But it was impossible that Christians should long continue to observe the whole Mosaic ritual, and the effort to do so was less and less consistently made."[12]

Despite Paul's teaching and the impossibility of keeping the law, there are still Christians who for one reason or another conscientiously place themselves under a small part of the law. Somehow, they find a plausible justification to bind them to a decree, yet readily ignore the observance of the rest of the law. Where is the scriptural guidance that permits such a selection? A long, hard look will show there is none. Just the opposite is what they will find. Paul in one of his many warnings to beware of Judaizers who wanted new Christians to become circumcised wrote, "And I testify again to every man who receives circumcision, that he is under obligation to keep the whole

---

12 George B. Stevens, Gospel and Law in the Teaching of Jesus Christ. *Searching Together,* Spring/Autumn 1992, 9-16.

Law" (Gal. 5:3). It is either all of the law or none of the law. Christian sects cannot have it both ways.

Christians who mix the Law with the Gospel or mix the Gospel with the Law are not "accurately handling the word of truth" (2 Tim. 2:15). "The Law is stern and rigorous; the Gospel is free and sweet. When the two are confused, an element of sternness is introduced into the Gospel, making it demanding, or an element of laxity is introduced into the Law making it more attainable."[13]

LAW AND GOSPEL ARE COMPLEMENTARY

The Law and Gospel are not opposites, nor are they the same. Each is evident in the other, but theologically they have differences. Despite that seeming dual dichotomy, "Both Testaments contain the revelation of one God, given to people who live by faith, are sustained by his grace, enjoy communion with Him as His covenant people, and persevere in faith."[14]

"We must study the distinction between Law and Gospel because in a real sense, Scripture presents us with nothing else."[15] With the Law, God's intention is to shut people up under disobedience and hold them accountable. Preaching must show people they are disobedient. It must show they have always been disobedient, cannot be anything but disobedient, and have no desire to be anything but disobedient. After hearing a good sermon on the Law, men recognize they do not want to do better. Follow that with the Gospel and men realize God wants to have mercy on them. "Law must be preached in its full rigor to make people guilty before God. Gospel must be preached in its full sweetness to make people righteous before God. If we try to do

13 Ritchie, 7-11.
14 John Murray, *Principles of Conduct* (Grand Rapids, Eerdmans, 1957), in *Five Views of Law and the Gospel*, Stanley N. Gundry, ed. (Grand Rapids: Zondervan, 1996), 16.
15 Ritchie, 7-11.

anything else with God's threats or promises, we are following our own agenda, and not God's."[16]

Kaiser makes another telling statement in *Five Views on Law and Gospel*. "The current evangelical generation has been raised almost devoid of any teaching on the place and use of the law in the life of the believer. This has resulted in a full (or perhaps semi-) antinomian approach to life. Is it any wonder that the unbelieving society around us is so lawless, if those who should have been light and salt to that same society were themselves not always sure what it was that they should be doing?"[17]

The Reformers were so certain of the importance of understanding the correct relationship between Law and Gospel they claimed that without it no one would be able to make sense out of Scripture. Martin Luther is reported to have said it was impossible to determine whether a person is a Christian, a Jew, or a pagan if they did not know and understand the distinction between Law and Gospel. "The true knowledge of the distinction between the Law and the Gospel is not only a glorious light, affording the correct understanding of the entire Holy Scriptures, but without this knowledge Scripture is and remains a sealed book."[18]

Nothing in this book intends to suggest the New Testament worship serves God's plan without the Old Testament. Equally important, nothing in this book means to imply the Old Testament manner of worship is better than the new covenant residing in the life, death, and resurrection of the Lord Jesus Christ.

If there is one overriding principle to this study, it is that God is holy, God's law is holy, and Jesus is the focus of the Law. Much of the

---

16 Ritchie, 7-11.
17 Walter C. Kaiser, Jr., response to *The Law is the Perfection of Righteousness in Jesus Christ: A Reformed Perspective* Willem A. VanGemeren in *Five views on Law and Gospel*, by Stanley N. Gundry. ed. (Grand Rapids: Zondervan, 1996), 75.
18 C. F. W. Walther, *The Proper Distinction Between Law and Gospel*. (St. Louis: Concordia Publishing House, 1986), 1.

misunderstanding this book attempts to explain is concentrated on the Lord Jesus as the focus of the Law. "For if you believed Moses, you would believe Me, for he wrote about Me. But if you do not believe his writings, how will you believe My words" (John 5:46–47)? The phrase "for he wrote about Me" is telling. It is an important testimony to the main subject of the Pentateuch (as well as the entire Old Testament) which is our Savior, the Lord Jesus Christ. Christians must never forget the only theme of the Bible is the redemption of mankind by Christ's sacrifice on Calvary. Keeping that thought in mind will provide clarity, not just for the Law and Gospel question, but also in any Bible study effort.

BIBLICIST VIEW OF SCRIPTURE

Much of the work available on Law and Gospel is disappointing. Readers face an either/or situation. Reformed theology and theonomy emphasize intertestamental continuity and subjection to the law, but dispensationalism and Lutheranism emphasize discontinuity and freedom. All four of these ideas were from fallible men. They are different; one must be wrong—or they all are wrong. Neither is it right in the sense that "God is not a God of confusion but of peace, as in all the churches of the saints" (1 Cor. 14:33). If scholars cannot settle the debate, imagine how confusing it must be for the layman.

The obvious question is how did this happen? Some scholar or many scholars misinterpreted a Scripture passage. Perhaps they misunderstood something another scholar wrote. Catholicism and many of the Reformers attempted to settle disputes and explain scriptural difficulties according to Greek philosophy. One mistake compounded another, and we have competing theology.

The goal of this book is to find as close to a biblical answer to the role of the law in the life of a New Testament Christian as possible. It was tempting to offer a critique of some the more egregious proof texts. That is not the point. Some academics maintain no scholarly work on a topic such as this is complete without some discussion on competing views. That is part of the problem. Competing views may come from the mind of man. Systems of theology created by men are not biblicist. The purely biblicist view wants only to know what the Scriptures say, not what men say. Other than the few necessary exceptions in chapter 10, there is no attempt to oppose, defend, or analyze the various views.

Willem A. VanGemeren made a profound statement that ought never to be far from the mind of a serious Bible student. He wrote, "Dispensational and Reformed theologians and exegetes may each cite texts in favor of their position, but the crux is Jesus' place in the whole of redemptive history. Since the revelation of God is in the Old Testament, the Old must be understood in the light of the Gospel of Jesus Christ. The opposite is also true. Since the Gospel of Christ is found in the Old Testament, the New Testament books must be seen in the light of the Old."[19]

First and arguably the most important prerequisite for interpreting Scripture is a desire for the truth. Next, there has to be dedication to the truth. This means exercising great care not to change or amplify the Word of God. Third, there must be diligence in ascertaining the truth. God's people need to search the Scriptures with a desire to stay with it until the truth is learned. Lastly, discernment is necessary. The serious Bible student must begin his study with prayer for the Holy Spirit to guide and close with prayer to comprehend the new learning and make it part of his life.

Correct hermeneutical principles are essential to correctly determining a biblicist view of Scripture. The most important is the common maxim of "context is king." Much of the error that leads to differing theological viewpoints comes from a method of interpretation that ignores "context is king." The careful student of Scripture

---

19 There is great, spiritually sound wisdom in VanGemeren's words. Despite what he writes, he does not hold true to what he says. He regularly cites proof texts to support his non-theonomic Reformed view of Law and Gospel. Willem A. VanGemeren. Response to *The Inauguration of the Law of Christ with the Gospel of Christ: A Dispensational View.* by Wayne Strickland in Gundry, Stanley N. ed. *Five Views of Law and the Gospel,* (Grand Rapids: Zondervan, 1996), 286.

observes five things: literary context, historical-cultural background, word meanings, grammatical relationships, and literary genre.

Several categories of biblical interpretation exist: allegorical, criticism, literal, and traditional or ecclesiastical methods. Literal is the only sound and safe approach to interpretation. It prevents runaway imaginations, sinful hearts, and traditional but unscriptural beliefs from distorting the meaning of a passage.

A biblicist view of Scripture uses the literal method. It is the normal, natural, intended sense of the biblical writer's choice of words and their meaning in context. It accepts the use of figures of speech, historical and geographical references, symbols, and types at face value. It relies on the ordinary use of words, grammar, and language. Use the single literal sense of a passage as well as the grammatico-historical approach to a text. Never look for a hidden meaning unknown to the author.

The interpretation has to concern itself with the intent of the biblical writer. Always examine the text of Scripture to seek the accurate intention of the author. John A. McLean firmly states, "Those who disregard authorial priority for reader response have already determined that they will be sovereign over the interpretation of the text and the intent of the original author."[20]

Frequently, the intention of the writer's focus is on the relationship between the Old Testament and the New Testament. Each New Testament passage that cites or refers to an Old Testament passage has a meaning in its own context in addition to the original statement of the Old Testament author. This method asserts that a text can have two referents—an historical figure and Christ in the same passage. The second referent in the New Testament reveals the light of completed revelation in Christ's fulfillment of the Old Testament. This method allows expanded meanings that naturally occur due to the progress of

---

20 John A. McLean, The Importance of Hermeneutics. In *The Fundamentals for the Twenty-first Century*, Mal Couch, ed. (Grand Rapids, MI: Kregel Publications, 2000), 77.

revelation through the Bible. It also does away with the problem of a difference in intent of the divine and human authors.

It is important to remember written words have the meaning understood by the author when written. Focus on the meaning of the word in the context in which it is written and used. Also, consider the use of the word in the culture at the time the biblical writers lived. Using context and culture together gives the reader protection from ascribing meanings to passages that are not present. A true biblicist retains "the distinctive message of the Bible according to the intent of its author while relating that message to the present world."[21]

Search for the principle involved. If an action such as foot washing is cultural, then it is not a required practice in worship services today. However, the principle Jesus taught is humility, which is important for every believer to exhibit.

Never use a verse just because a few words strengthen a point in a sermon or a theological system. Always read what becomes before and after the verse. If the passage does not support the point, then find another passage. If no supporting passage that supports a sermon point is available, then stop. Such efforts to find a proof text are academically and spiritually bankrupt. If proof-texting is necessary to substantiate a position, Christendom is better off if that position does not see the light of day. The researcher is on a wrong track and ought to start over and get it right.

"Only in a holistic, canonical approach to interpreting Scripture can we begin to derive the richness, the depth, the wisdom and splendor there is to be found in the plan of God."[22] Never look at the Old Testament as preparatory, or teach and preach with the new superimposed over the old.

21 Michael Harding, Preserved for Proclamation and Transformation, In God's Word in our Hands. James B. Williams, ed. (Greenville, SC: Ambassador-Emerald International 2003), 346.
22 Kaiser, 58.

The scholar may come across topics that God has chosen not to reveal. There are instances in both Testaments of God hiding something from believers. Daniel 12:4, 9 relates how God explained to Daniel that a vision would remain sealed until fulfilled when men would understand. After the seven thunders, a voice from heaven told John to "Seal up the things which the seven peals of thunder have spoken and do not write them" (Rev. 10:4). God has not revealed everything about Himself and His plan for Creation, only those things that He desires us to know. We do not know the rest, nor do we need to know and should not concern ourselves with what He keeps hidden. Accept it as not for us. Do not try to manufacture something about what God did not intend for men to know. God will reveal the answer when He wants us to know. Never forget who we are in our relationship with God. He can keep secrets from us, His creation, if He desires. "God's revealed will is that which we must carry out."[23]

To obtain a biblicist view of Scripture, always exercise caution in four key areas when interpreting the Scriptures.

- Avoid strict, unalterable adherence to traditional beliefs. Theological beliefs of denominationalism can be so pervasive that readers will be unable to see the truth of a passage. This can alter true interpretation of Scripture.

- Experiences and feelings are unreliable because they are fleshly emotions. Heavily emotional interpretation blocks objective rendering of a passage. Individual experiences such as *it works for me so it must be true* or *this verse blessed me so it is valid for all* lead to skewed interpretations.

- Never evaluate a passage in purely mental terms. Always seek the guidance of the Holy Spirit or use the accepted body of doctrine. Bible study without sensitivity to the leading of the Holy Spirit

---

23 Albert Barnes, *Notes on the Old Testament, Explanatory and Practical, vol. Exodus – Ruth.* ed. Robert Frew, 16th printing. (Grand Rapids, MI: Baker Book House, 1949, reprint 1978), 329.

will lead to insufficient understanding of the passage. Study without prayer often leads to meanings that match false beliefs and prejudices. Worse, the result may be theologically liberal or simply wrong. In nearly every such effort, the interpretation ignores context and doctrine.

- Never take a verse by itself at face value. Always read and study it in context of what comes before and after as well as the history and circumstances of the passage. This will prevent proof-texting where anything can mean whatever the teacher wants.

The Bible is the source from which Christians find their theology. It is the only objective standard. The careful Bible teacher will not teach his students to follow a system of theology. He will teach them to become a biblicist. He will teach them to know their Bible. He will teach them God's Word.

CHAPTER 2

MATTHEW 5:17–20

IN MATTHEW 5:17-20, CHRIST IS answering criticism that He is minimizing the Mosaic Law. Because He was a teacher who opposed the corrupt religious establishment of the scribes and Pharisees, many people thought He wanted to abolish the customs of the nation. The scribes and Pharisees accused Him of wanting to destroy the Law they so religiously followed. In this passage, Jesus explains that is not His purpose. He teaches that He came to carry out the Law. Coming events, His death and resurrection, show that He did so by perfectly fulfilling all the types and prophecies found in the Old Testament. He obeyed the Law perfectly and fulfilled in Himself everything the prophets had spoken. Ultimately, He fulfilled the Law for the Jews as well as all mankind.

D. Martyn Lloyd-Jones writes of there being two great pronouncements in these four verses. In the first pronouncement, verses 17 and 18, Jesus is telling the crowd "that everything He is going to teach is in absolute harmony with the entire teaching of the Old Testament Scriptures." In the second pronouncement, verses 19 and 20, Jesus explains that His teaching, which is in perfect harmony with the Old Testament, "is in complete disharmony with, and an utter contradiction of, the teaching of the Pharisees and scribes."[1]

In essence, Jesus was trying to show that living in accordance with true religion is different from living in strict obedience to the

---

1 D. Martyn Lloyd-Jones, *Studies in the Sermon on the Mount.* (Grand Rapids, MI: William B. Eerdmans Publishing Company, 1976), 158.

Law. This passage shows that "Christ's coming revealed completely the purpose and meaning of the Old Testament."[2] It also explains how the nation and its people should view the religion of the day.

VERSE 17[3]

"Think not that I am come to destroy the law, or the prophets: I am not come to destroy, but to fulfill" (KJV).

"Do not think that I came to abolish the Law or the Prophets; I did not come to abolish but to fulfill" (NASB).

Verse 17 is a short verse, but it has a great many implications for Christians in their understanding of the Bible. In some Christian circles, the teaching of this verse leaves out the full import of Christ's words. It receives lip service as merely fulfilling all the types, shadows, and prophecies of the longed for Messiah. This chapter will show these few words mean so much more. A proper understanding of this verse will reveal much about the Scriptures and God's plan of the ages.

In the Greek, the word *think* means to suppose. The word translated *destroy* or *abolish* means to overthrow completely. Jesus is telling his listeners that concerning the Law, do not suppose He is coming to abolish, destroy, or overthrow the Law. His purpose was "not to subvert, abrogate, or annul, but to establish the Law and the prophets—to unfold them, to embody them in living form, and to enshrine them in the reverence, affection, and character of men."[4] He declared His purpose to fulfill the Law in order to make four statements:

2 James M. Gray, *Christians Workers' Bible Commentary.* (Westwood, NJ: Fleming H. Revell Company, 1953), 298.
3 The principle Bible translation used in this book is the New American Standard Bible. Even so, this chapter uses many familiar King James Version words and phrases because readers know them well. Each verse heading in this chapter opens with both the KJV and NASB rendering of the text.
4 Robert Jamieson, A.R. Fausset, David Brown, *Commentary: Practical and Explanatory on the Whole Bible,* new and rev. ed. (Grand Rapids, Michigan: Zondervan, 1961), 899.

- To God-fearing Jews living in obedience to God, do not worry; I am not going to destroy the foundation of your faith. Do not think that men are free from the obligation of obeying the commands of God. They cannot live as they please.

- To those who expected the Messiah to be a military leader to overthrow Roman rule, I am not here to lead a revolutionary movement.

- To the hypocritical religious leaders who pretend great reverence for the Law—do not waste your time trying to find something in my teachings that is contrary to God's revelation of Himself to mankind. It is not there.

- To worldly Jews in Christ's day (to atheists and agnostics today), who have a distaste for the things of God and are weary of that yoke, I am come to relieve you of your obligation to obey a list of rules. I am come to grant mercy and grace so you can live a life of faith.

The word *fulfill* is important. Usually, scholars translate the Greek word to mean complete.[5] Here it demands more. It has the idea of to satisfy, to execute an office, or to finish a task. Jesus' intention was to finish or carry out the sayings and prophecies of the Old Testament. Indeed, He opened His public ministry by reading from Isaiah 61:1–2, "The Spirit of the Lord GOD is upon me, because the LORD has anointed me to bring good news to the afflicted; He has sent me to bind up the brokenhearted, to proclaim liberty to captives and freedom to prisoners; to proclaim the favorable year of the Lord and the day of vengeance of our God; to comfort all who mourn." Luke 4:18–19 recounts His reading of Isaiah, but His statement in Luke 4:21 is most significant: "This day is this Scripture fulfilled in your ears." Christ came to make good the promises of the Law, and the predictions of

---

5 Greg L. Bahnsen argues the sense in which Christ fulfilled the law is best understood by the translation "to confirm." A response to *The Inauguration of the Law of Christ with the Gospel of Christ: A Dispensational View* by Wayne Strickland in Gundry, Stanley N. ed. *Five Views of Law and the Gospel*, (Grand Rapids: Zondervan, 1996), 298.

the prophets, all of which bore witness of His coming and work for the salvation for mankind. "You search the Scriptures because you think that in them you have eternal life; it is these that testify about Me" (John 5:39). "These were to be fulfilled and fully accomplished by His life and sufferings."[6]

The Law of Moses contained numerous sacrifices and rituals that foreshadowed the coming Messiah. All of these sacrifices and rituals found fulfillment in His coming and sacrifice on Calvary. Christ gave "full obedience to the law, literally fulfilling everything said and stated in the law and the prophets."[7]

The Prophets and the Writings contained untold numbers of predictions concerning His coming, His life, and His death. The words of the Prophets and the Writings were an exposition of the law. The Prophets taught the law to show how people ought to live in order to please God. Their predictions amplified and explained all the types and shadows. Christ's life established "the absolute and final meaning of the law and the prophets."[8] Three times in his sermon in Acts 3, Peter indicated that all the Old Testament prophets pointed forward to Jesus:

"But the things which God announced beforehand by the mouth of all the prophets, that His Christ would suffer, He has thus fulfilled" (3:18).

"Whom heaven must receive until *the* period of restoration of all things about which God spoke by the mouth of His holy prophets from ancient time" (3:21).

6 Albert Barnes, *Notes on the New Testament, Explanatory and Practical*, vol. Matthew and Mark. ed. Robert Frew, 16th printing. (Grand Rapids, MI: Baker Book House, 1949, reprint 1978), 49.
7 Lloyd-Jones, 162.
8 A. Lukyn Williams, Matthew, vol. 1 in *The Pulpit Commentary*, ed. H.D.M. Spence & Joseph Exell. (New York: Funk & Wagnalls, 1913), 155.

"And likewise, all the prophets who have spoken, from Samuel
and *his* successors onward, also announced these days" (3:24).

God is the author of both Testaments. The Jews readily accepted
that the Law, the Prophets, and the Writings came from God. They had
experienced their power and purity. In a discussion with the religious
leaders concerning His authority, Jesus said, "For if you believed Moses,
you would believe Me, for he wrote about Me. But if you do not believe
his writings, how will you believe My words" (John 5:46–47)? With that
statement, Christ placed His authority in the Pentateuch.

The Lord Jesus Christ is the primary subject of the Old
Testament. It contains more than one hundred specific prophecies
concerning His reason for coming to earth. If men disregard the
writings of the Old Testament, they disregard the Lord and His
purpose at Calvary. The work Christ came to do cannot take away
the authority of the Scriptures.

Christ gave no command in His time on earth that violated the
law of nature or the Mosaic Law; nor did He forbid anything that
those laws had required. It is a great mistake to think He does. In His
omniscience, Jesus knew there would be some Jews and others in the
Church Age who would misunderstand what He meant in His tribute
to John the Baptist, "For all the prophets and the Law prophesied until
John" (Matt. 11:13). He did not mean the Old Testament ended with John.
He meant that what the prophets had foretold as coming has come. The
Law and the Prophets were instructors concerning the Christ. John's
preaching showed that all the predictions of the Messiah, the types
and ceremonies, were now about to be fully and finally accomplished,
for the Messiah was here. Jesus takes care to prevent any misunderstanding that He intended nullify the Old Testament with the words,
"I did not come to abolish."

He came to fulfill the Law and the Prophets. He could do nothing else but obey the commands of the Law, for "when the fullness
of the time came, God sent forth His Son, born of a woman, born

under the Law" (Gal. 4:4). "Though He is eternally above it, as Son of God He came and was made under the Law, as one who had to carry it out."[9] In no other way does God signify the importance of the law better than with this fact—God placed His Son under the law. In everything, He was obedient to the law. He honored his parents, sanctified the Sabbath, prayed, gave alms, and did that which no one else could—He obeyed the law perfectly. He never broke the law in anything.

What Christ came to establish exactly agreed with the Law, the Prophets, and the Writings. The prophets were commentators upon the Law, and together they made up the rule of faith and practice, which the Jews commonly observed. The Savior's new teachings did not replace the Mosaic Law, nor did they absorb it. Instead, His teachings fully developed the Mosaic Law. The entire theme of the Old Testament and the New Testament is the Lord Jesus Christ and the redemption He makes possible for all mankind. "What purpose other than this proclamation does Scripture have from beginning to end? Messiah, God's Son, was to come and through His sacrifice, as an innocent Lamb of God, bear and remove the sins of the world and thus redeem men from eternal death for eternal salvation. For the sake of Messiah and God's son, Holy Scripture was written, and for His sake everything that happened took place."[10]

The Old Testament, including the Law, used by Jesus and the apostles, has a place in Christian living. God established it. Man cannot take His words lightly, no matter how old they are. The Law contains practical truths of an eternal nature. It has a moral character that is a timeless reference for the behavior of men. It has a spiritual benefit that uplifts men. The Law is not just a guideline; it is the Word of God: it pointed to the Lord Jesus Christ who fulfilled it.

---

9 Lloyd-Jones, 1976), 167.
10 Martin Luther, *What Luther Says*, compiled by Ewald M. Plass (St. Louis: Concordia, 1959, vol. 1), 69.

VERSE 18

"For verily I say unto you, Till heaven and earth pass, one jot
or one tittle shall in no wise pass from the law, till all be
fulfilled" (KJV).

"For truly I say to you, until heaven and earth pass away, not
the smallest letter or stroke shall pass from the Law until
all is accomplished" (NASB).

Before beginning an exegesis of verse 18, it is necessary to define
several key words and phrases.

For

Greek speakers use the word translated *for* when they intend to
make a firm statement with the need to assign a reason. Its common
use is in an argument or debate as a forceful stressing of a critical
point. It is similar to the emphatic use of the English phrase "without
a doubt" with the idea of no doubt whatsoever.

Truly (Verily in KJV)

Readers see the word *verily* so much they give it little thought.
Verily is the Hebrew word *amēn*. It is a transliteration of the Hebrew
word *truth* often used as an interjection, meaning "so be it." In Greek
usage, it came to mean a solemn or emphatic declaration or statement.
In English, the word transliterates into *amen*, which, as used today,
serves to support and endorse prayer or praise.

The early church used *amen* in a continuation of a worship form
of the Hebrews. Its meaning denotes "the faithful God" (Deut. 7:9) or
"the God of truth" (Isa. 65:16). By extension, if God is faithful, then his
testimonies and precepts are sure. Thus, when referring to something
said by God, verily (or amen) means, "It is and shall be so."

When said by men, *amen* is defined as, "So let it be." Men have used amen to express their agreement to a law and their willingness to assent to the penalties of breaking it. Christians also use it to express acquiescence to another's prayer. In this context the definition is "let God say so too."

"Jesus gives the word a new use by prefixing it to His statements to give them weight and solemnity."[11] Used here in reference to the Mosaic Law, it is an expression of supreme legislative authority.[12] No higher claim to divine authority is possible. It is Jehovah's exclusive prerogative to give laws to men; "You are to perform My judgments and keep My statutes, to live in accord with them; I am the Lord your God. So you shall keep My statutes and My judgments, by which a man may live if he does them; I am the Lord" (Lev. 18:4-5).

"In No Wise"

The phrase *no wise* is a double negative in the Greek. It strongly expresses an emphatic no. Its equivalent in today's English is "Absolutely not!"

Jot and Tittle

A jot is the smallest letter in the Hebrew alphabet, something like the lower case letter *i*. A tittle denotes a small stroke, which distinguishes certain Hebrew letters from others. It means "a little horn" and is a small protrusion on letters much like the serif in many fonts that widens a letter at the top and bottom. It is similar in appearance to a comma, but placed at the top of a letter. Its presence or absence determines the meaning of a letter.

The rabbis attached great importance to a tittle, which gives impact to the Lord using jot and tittle together to express the fact that not a

---

11 J. Newton Davies, Matthew in *The Abingdon Bible Commentary*. Frederick C. Eiselen, Edwin Lewis, and David G. Downey ed. (New York: Abingdon-Cokesbury Press, 1929), 963.
12 Jamieson, 899.

single item of the Law, not even a small insignificant letter or stroke, will pass away or remain unfulfilled.

God revealed the prophetic plan of the Old Testament to point to Christ. He does not intend that any of it be set aside. Even the smallest letter or the smallest mark will not be removed because it is all part of God's plan. "The word of the Lord endures forever both the Word of the Law, and that of the Gospel. The care of God concerning His law extends itself even to those things that seem to be of least account in it, the jots and the tittles; for whatever belongs to God, and bears his stamp, be it ever so little, it shall be preserved."[13] With His use of jot and tittle, it is clear that "Jesus Christ believed that the Bible was the supreme authority over life."[14]

If God considers such a small detail as the shape of letters important, who is man to ignore any part of His Word? Man cannot disregard so much as one single, tiny detail of the authority of the Bible. Men must never forget that God's Word, both Old Testament and New Testament, is eternal and contains absolute truth. We accord the Bible great respect because it is the very Words of God, His revelation of Himself to mankind. Writing under the inspiration of the Holy Spirit, Paul penned these words about the Old Testament and the Law: "All Scripture is inspired by God and profitable for teaching, for reproof, for correction, for training in righteousness" (2 Tim. 3:16). The word *all* means every single bit of the Bible is important, worthy of study, and a guide for living.

Fulfill

The Greek word translated *fulfill* in the KJV (accomplished, NASB) has many nuances and multiple meanings, thus is a source of many scholarly arguments. It has the idea of to come into being or to take

---

13 Matthew Henry's Complete Commentary on the Whole Bible. Public Domain. This text is from the Christian Classics Ethereal Library located at www.ccel. org. (Tempe, AZ: The Crosswire Software and Bible Society). Commentary on Matthew 5:18.
14 James Montgomery Boice, *The Sermon on the Mount.* (Grand Rapids, MI, Baker Books, 1972), 74.

place. The sense of this passage is "until all is accomplished."[15] The law will not have even the smallest loss of validity or authority. Jamieson, Fausset, and Brown give the phrase *till all be fulfilled* a meaning of "it *shall* be had in undiminished and enduring honor, from its greatest to its least requirements."[16]

What Jesus Said

Jesus said in verse 18, "Without a doubt, here is a truth, not until heaven, the eternal dwelling place of God and the whole world, including the occupants, perishes absolutely nothing in the law, even the smallest, most minute letter or mark will perish. The Law, the Prophets, and the Writings, the entire Word of God, will last until the end of time that marks this earthly existence." Then, at the end of time, will be the final accomplishment of the things prophesied in the Old Testament law and further explained and advanced in the New Testament gospel. The Lord Jesus Christ will carry out the prophecies, types, and shadows to completion.

VERSE 19

"Whosoever therefore shall break one of these least commandments, and shall teach men so, he shall be called the least in the kingdom of heaven: but whosoever shall do and teach them, the same shall be called great in the kingdom of heaven" (KJV).

"Whoever then annuls one of the least of these commandments, and teaches others *to do* the same, shall be called least in the kingdom of heaven; but whoever keeps and teaches *them*, he shall be called great in the kingdom of heaven" (NASB).

---

15 That is the rendering in the NASB, ESV, ASV, AMP, and several other modern translations.
16 Jamieson, 899.

Jesus is speaking of the misuse of the Mosaic Law. "The law was never intended to be the focus or the end in itself."[17] Religious leaders focused on details of the Law and elevated them to a status that led to a misapplication of the rites and ceremonies. This in turn led to a cold, dead religion that, when practiced, eliminated true worship of God.

Before addressing the misuse of the law, there is a need for a brief explanation of the phrase *kingdom of heaven*. The kingdom of heaven is the same as the kingdom of God used in the other synoptic Gospels. There have been numerous ill-advised efforts to assign different meanings to the two terms. The two terms are synonymous and interchangeable.[18] The proof of this is quite simple. When Mark and Luke relate their version of an event in Matthew, they use the term *kingdom of God*. Matthew wrote to Jews who feared to utter the name of God. Thus, he nearly always used the term *kingdom of heaven*. It "was the central theme of the preaching and teaching of Jesus. It refers to the visible manifestation of God's reign over the universe."[19]

The kingdom of heaven was a present kingdom while Christ was on earth. "But if I cast out demons by the Spirit of God, then the kingdom of God has come upon you" (Matt. 12:28). "Since he does not cast out by Satan, he must cast out by the power of God, and therefore his actions demonstrated the potential arrival of the kingdom of God."[20] Christ casting out demons is actually an act of destruction of the kingdom of Satan. It implies the setting up of the kingdom of heaven.

It is important to recognize there are both a present kingdom and a coming kingdom in order to understand the intent of *kingdom of heaven*.

---

17 Willem A. VanGemeren, *The Law is the Perfection of Righteousness in Jesus Christ: A Reformed Perspective*. in Gundry, Stanley N. ed. *Five Views of Law and the Gospel*, (Grand Rapids: Zondervan, 1996), 19.

18 Compare Matt. 19:23–24 with Mark 10:23–24, Matt. 13:11 with Mark 4:11, Matt. 13:31 with Mark 4:30–31, Matt. 13:33 with Luke 13:20–21, Matt. 18:3 with Mark 10:15, Matt. 19:14 with Mark 10:14, and Matt. 8:11–12 with Luke 13:28–29.

19 William C. Martin, *The Layman's Bible Encyclopedia*. (Nashville: The Southwestern Co., 1964), 446.

20 J.W. McGarvey, and Philip Y. Pendleton, *The Fourfold Gospel and Commentary on Acts of Apostles*. (Tempe, AZ: The Crosswire Software and Bible Society, 1863, 1882).

The kingdom is in the future; we pray, "Thy kingdom come" (Matt. 6:10). Paul looked forward to a coming kingdom, "I solemnly charge you in the presence of God and of Christ Jesus, who is to judge the living and the dead, and by His appearing and His kingdom" (2 Tim. 4:1). God's people can have confidence they will enjoy the coming kingdom, "*For in this way the entrance into the eternal kingdom of our Lord and Savior Jesus Christ will be abundantly supplied to you*" (2 Pet. 1:11).

Antinomianism Destroyed

The phrase *shall break* in the KJV (annuls, NASB) is not the opposite of obey. It has the idea of abolish or annul. The Greek word translated *commandments* denotes, in general, an injunction, a charge, or to moral and religious precepts.[21] The idea is not that of making a mistake while trying to live obediently to the Law. Instead, it means to abolish a portion of the Law, to remove it, or to disregard a portion of the Law as unimportant. That is antinomianism, the idea that the gospel frees Christians from required obedience to any law, whether scriptural, civil, or moral. Antinomians contend that under the gospel dispensation of grace, the Old Testament law is of no use or obligation because faith alone and the gift of divine grace is all that is necessary for salvation.

Here Christ destroyed antinomian thinking forever. He refutes the heresy that Christians do not have to follow well-established biblical instructions, relying only on faith and divine grace. Grace is necessary to obey the law, but dependence on grace without obeying the law is wrong. "All of the details—down to the least letter of the least commandment—are binding until the end of the universe."[22] "That the 'least of these commandments' referred to by our Lord are those set forth in the Pentateuch, and not merely those of the 'moral law' or

---

21 William. E. Vine, *An Expository Dictionary of Old Testament Words.* Edited by F. F. Bruce. (Old Tappan, NJ: Fleming H. Revell Co., 1978), 212.

22 Greg L. Bahnsen, response to *The Law of Christ as the Fulfillment of the Law of Moses: A Modified Lutheran View* by Douglas J. Moo in Gundry, Stanley N. ed. *Five Views of Law and the Gospel*, (Grand Rapids: Zondervan, 1996), 387.

the few contained in the Sermon on the Mount, is perfectly clear from the context. He is speaking about the entire law of Moses."[23]

Two Teachers

Jesus compares two different teachers in verse 19, both of whom are believers. He is leading up to verse 20 where He speaks of the scribes and Pharisees who had added tradition to the Law. The first teacher is one who destroys even the smallest precept of the Law and instructs other men in such a manner that will lead them to break the Law. Pharisaic tradition had become elevated to a status that was greater than the law God gave to Moses. "The legalistic rituals of which the Pharisees were so fond were corruptions of types of the real things that were to come in Christ."[24] The importance of the Mosaic ceremonies lay in their showing a truth about the coming Messiah. The legalistic additions contain nothing that will edify worshippers or show the way to a life of victory in Christ. Instead, their only purpose is to edify men, giving them a false sense of comfort and security in a hopeless religion of works without faith.

Of course, this principle also includes any Christian who teaches and preaches any doctrine in any era that is not the true gospel. Jesus is speaking to God's people, believers who have trusted the Lord as Savior. He gives a warning that has both a present and a future meaning. The preacher or teacher who disregards any part of the Law will have a degraded and inferior state in the present stage of the kingdom of heaven. They will experience divine retribution and have the same condition of dishonor they have brought to the truth of the Word of God.

In the future kingdom, those who added to or took away from the Law, the Word of God, will have diminished status because their disobedient hearts do not reflect the character that God demands. Paul writes of the worst case, "Each man's work will become evident; for the day will show it because it is *to be* revealed with fire, and the fire

23 Alva J. McClain, *Law and Grace*. 1954. Reprint, (Chicago: Moody Press, 1967), 9.
24 Merrill F. Unger, *Unger's Bible Handbook*. (Chicago: Moody Press, 1966), 696.

itself will test the quality of each man's work. If any man's work which he has built on it remains, he will receive a reward. If any man's work is burned up, he will suffer loss; but he himself will be saved, yet so as through fire" (1 Cor. 3:13–15).

The second teacher Jesus mentions is one who can successfully live the Law, as well as instruct others how to live and obey the Law. Jesus is referring to a teacher whose efforts exalt the authority and honor of God's law. This teacher explains that all the Law is important and takes care not to specify that any part of the Law is more important than any other portion. That one will have the same position of honor and authority to which they exalt the Word of God. So important is the Law, that even a conscious effort to obey a small commandment of the Law coupled with trying to spread it will earn that person a high position in the kingdom of heaven.

Application of Verse 19

Believers can learn several things from this verse:

- All the law of God is important. Every believer ought to honor it just as Christ did.

- A true believer respects all the commandments of God.

- One should preach and teach all commands of God.

- Anyone who thinks there are any Laws of God they need not obey are unworthy of the kingdom of heaven.

God's people who take the Scriptures seriously ought to pray with the psalmist, "You have ordained Your precepts, that we should keep *them* diligently. Oh that my ways may be established to keep Your statutes! Then I shall not be ashamed when I look upon all Your commandments" (Ps. 119:4–6). Adding to or taking away from the Law is anathema: "You shall not add to the word which I am commanding you, nor take away from it, that you may keep the commandments of the Lord your God which I command you" (Deut. 4:2).

VERSE 20

"For I say unto you, that except your righteousness shall exceed the righteousness of the scribes and Pharisees, ye shall in no case enter into the kingdom of heaven" (KJV).

"For I say to you that unless your righteousness surpasses *that* of the scribes and Pharisees, you will not enter the kingdom of heaven" (NASB).

Scribes and Pharisees

Scribes devoted their lives to the study the law. They copied the Scriptures, exercising great care for accuracy. They became recognized authorities on Mosaic Law because they knew the Scriptures in minute detail. Over time, their role evolved into that of a lawyer. Scribes became very influential and usually allied with the Pharisees. Over time, their function regarding the law shifted into teaching and using it in connection with the Sanhedrin and various local courts. The decisions of the leading scribes became oral law or "tradition." In their regime, true religion became little more than external formalism, and their traditions changed the law from being a help in moral and spiritual life into an obstacle that prevented true access to God. Christ had harsh words for them: "Woe to you lawyers! For you have taken away the key of knowledge; you yourselves did not enter, and you hindered those who were entering" (Luke 11:52).

The name Pharisee means "separatist." They were a religious group founded in reaction to Jews who were accepting Greek culture. Their aim was to preserve national integrity and strict conformity to Mosaic Law. As a religious group, they set themselves apart from ordinary living. It was not until much later that they developed into self-righteous and hypocritical formalists. Over the years, they created 613 extra-biblical rules to guide them in their daily living. These additional rules had the purpose of protecting them from offending the law of God. Gradually, their manmade rules took on greater and greater importance until the rules achieved equal status to the God-given law. They practically deified the Law with their rules. Their emphasis was not upon the righteousness of an action, but upon its formal correctness. Their strict interpretation sometimes alienated them from fellow Jews as well as the heathen. They are a classic case of loyalty to truth producing excessive pride and hypocrisy where they continually justified themselves before men. They trusted in their system and felt they had no need of a Savior. Jesus, who knew their hearts, was well aware "they were polluted, full of iniquity, and spiritually dead."[25] He regularly denounced the perversion of their ideology. "Their opposition to Christ is inevitable; His manner of life and teaching was essentially a condemnation of theirs; hence his denunciation of them."[26]

Righteousness Contrasted

Greek speakers used the word translated to the opening word *for* when they intend to make a firm statement with the need to assign a reason. Its common use is in an argument or debate as a forceful stressing of a critical point. It is similar to the emphatic use of the English phrase *without a doubt,* with the idea of no doubt whatsoever. In this instance, it leads to an explanation of the warning contained in verse 19.

Righteousness refers to whatever is right or just in itself that also conforms to the revealed will of God. "It is used to denote an attribute of God, the context of which shows that 'the righteousness of God'

---

25 Greg L. Bahnsen, *The Theonomic Reformed Approach to Law and Gospel,* in Gundry, Stanley N. ed. *Five Views of Law and the Gospel,* (Grand Rapids: Zondervan, 1996), 95.
26 Vine, 863.

means essentially the same as His faithfulness, His truthfulness, that which is consistent with His own nature and promises."[27]

The phrase "your righteousness" identifies a difference between that of the scribes and Pharisees and true believers. The righteousness of the scribes and Pharisees consisted of a mere outward, unspiritual conformity to the Mosaic code, though they observed it scrupulously.[28] So mechanical had their religion become that they were able to honor God with their actions and disgrace Him with their lives. Their observance of the rites of Judaism was religious perfection. At the same time, they wallowed in selfish indulgence and immorality. That is the reason the scribes and Pharisees walked away in shameful silence when Jesus "said unto them, 'He who is without sin among you, let him *be the* first to throw a stone at her'" (John 8:7), concerning the woman taken in adultery. Their self-righteous facade collapsed when confronted with true righteousness.

The ceremonial aspect of the law was more important to the Pharisees than its guidance of morality. Their own words condemn them. "The Pharisees and the scribes asked Him, 'Why do Your disciples not walk according to the tradition of the elders, but eat their bread with impure hands'" (Mark 7:5)? Like the papists, they placed manmade tradition higher than true heartfelt love and obedience to God. Jesus responded by calling them hypocrites. He quoted Isaiah 29:13, "This people honors Me with their lips, but their heart is far away from Me" (Mark 7:6).

The scribes and Pharisees were more concerned with outward appearances than the inward condition of the heart. They complained to Jesus because the disciples once sat down to eat without washing. Jesus responded by saying, "Do you not understand that everything that goes into the mouth passes into the stomach, and is eliminated? But the things that proceed out of the mouth come from the heart,

27 Vine, 980.
28 Homer A. Kent, *Matthew* in *The Wycliffe Bible Commentary*, ed. Charles F. Pfeiffer and Everett F. Harrison. (Nashville: The Southwestern Co., 1962), 937.

and those defile the man" (Matt. 15:17–18). What men say and do comes from the heart and reveals their true nature.

The scribes and Pharisees "worked by traditions, and most of these traditions were really nothing but very clever and subtle ways of evading the demands of the law."[29] They avoided these demands by observing the law in a manner of their own creation. That justified their disobedience in a worldly cloak of religiosity. The form of worship of the religious professionals did not please God. Everything they did was to promote their own glory, to elevate themselves in the eyes of the public, to satisfy their selfish egos. Nothing they did glorified God, "But they do all their deeds to be noticed by men" (Matt. 23:5).

In Matthew 23, Jesus delivers a stinging indictment of the scribes and Pharisees. Seven times He calls them hypocrites, five times he calls them blind, and fools twice. He called them serpents, a generation of vipers. The illusion to the serpent in the Garden is inescapable. With poisonous tongues they deceived men with a form of religion that was an evil cancer from their "father the devil" (John 8:44).

Christ called them "whited sepulchers, which indeed appear beautiful outward, but are within full of dead *men's* bones, and of all uncleanness" (Matt. 23:27, KJV). He dismissed Pharisees as little more than a beautiful tombstone over a box of decaying flesh and bones.

The contrast with the Pharisee's righteousness is true righteousness, which depends upon men having the character that God demands. "Our righteousness then—if it is to contrast with the outward, formal, phony righteousness of the scribes and Pharisees—must be inward, vital, and spiritual."[30] Our righteousness must be over and above; indeed, it must abound over that of the scribes and Pharisees. "He saved us, not on the basis of deeds which we have done in righteousness, but according to His mercy, by the washing of regeneration and renewing by the Holy Spirit" (Titus 3:5).

---

29 Lloyd-Jones, 179.
30 Jamieson, 900.

The two words *no case* in the KJV are another double negative similar to the "no wise" in verse 18, though here it is stronger. It powerfully expresses an emphatic negation, "by no means," or "absolutely in every instance no!" They "will not enter the kingdom of heaven." Again, there is a present and a future implication. If we have the righteousness of the scribes and Pharisees, then we are members of the present kingdom of heaven only in name. Jesus is saying that unless a person has more holiness of character than the scribes and Pharisees, they cannot be a believer and have no chance of participating in the present kingdom nor have any hope of enjoying the future kingdom. In effect, Jesus is saying, "Without a doubt, your righteousness must be far greater than that of the scribes and Pharisees, or there is absolutely no way you will see the kingdom of heaven!"[31]

Gamaliel and Saul of Tarsus were very earnest, very righteous, and very serious Jews. Their every action revealed an intense, overriding zealousness concerning the Law. Their actions were good, but their hearts were without love and filled with evil. Their religious formalism did not produce fruit. No amount of slavish devotion to keeping the Law and their rules could prepare them for the kingdom of heaven. The Pharisees equated blamelessness in the law as equivalent to salvation. The phony righteousness of the scribes and Pharisees was insufficient to be a part of the kingdom of heaven.

Before the Damascus Road experience, Paul was a member of that lofty group of self-righteous rule makers. Afterwards, he knew true righteousness. The Apostle, who was certainly in a position to know, explained the inadequacy of the righteousness of the Pharisees in Philippians 3:4–9. Paul showed how many Jews had confidence in their standing as a Jew. They believed they could earn salvation through the law. He explains that if anyone can make that claim, he can. Paul could trace his genealogy back to Jacob. He was born an Israelite, the privileged line that goes back to the promise given by God. His mention

---

31 The author's modern English rendering of verse twenty.

of the tribe of Benjamin was an allusion to super spirituality. The tribe of Benjamin, along with Judah, is one of only two tribes that stayed faithful when the nation split after Solomon. The northern border of the tribe touched the Temple. They were close to the house of God and all the religious rites that took place there. Paul was a Pharisee, the best and most spiritual of the Jews. If there are any good Hebrews, then he was above them all. Like the rich young ruler, Paul, in the flesh, obeyed all the rules from his youth (Matt. 19:20, Mark 10:20, Luke 18:21). His zeal was unquestioned. He reminds them that he went from house to house seeking out and persecuting Christians who violated the rules of the Pharisees.

The point Paul is trying to make is that if anyone was capable of earning salvation from being a Pharisee, he is that man. Paul explained to the Philippians that all his earthly accomplishments are worthless, nothing but dung. He threw his heritage as a Pharisee away because it was fleshly, worldly, and of no value. There is a new and better way, a living way. The Lord Jesus Christ made all his Pharisaical works unnecessary. No one can earn salvation in the flesh. No earthly effort of man is sufficient for salvation. Jesus Christ is worth giving up everything in order to know Him. Everything else is worthless when compared to the surpassing value of knowing Jesus Christ as Lord. Every religious act is worthless, nothing but waste, unless it leads to Christ. Christ is the object of our devotion, the source of our salvation, the hope of our future.

True Righteousness

Jesus does not mean that righteous Christians must "painfully toil through the various enactments, ceremonial and other, of the Law as the scribes and Pharisees did, only with more serious and earnest purpose."[32] The Pharisees could not do it, and they tried with great sincerity. The scribes could not do it, and they were experts who knew the Law better than other men.

32 Williams, 158.

That was the reason for the Jerusalem Council where the apostles debated whether Gentiles had to obey the strictures of the ceremonial law before accepting them into the Christian religion. Peter said, "Now therefore why do you put God to the test by placing upon the neck of the disciples a yoke which neither our fathers nor we have been able to bear" (Acts 15:10)? The Jews could not fully obey the Law, why expect the Gentile Christians to be able to do so?

The real question here is what kind of righteousness will satisfy the requirements to enter the kingdom of heaven? We find the answer in Jesus' response to Nicodemus. "Truly, truly, I say to you, unless one is born again he cannot see the kingdom of God" (John 3:3). Men must be born again of the Spirit in order to enter the kingdom. Paul adds, "For with the heart a person believes, resulting in righteousness, and with the mouth he confesses, resulting in salvation" (Rom. 10:10). Following the rebirth true believers are able to make a public profession of their heart change.

The righteousness necessary to enter the kingdom of heaven is manifest by "purity, chastity, honesty, self-control, the fear of God, and the love of man. It is pure, eternal, and makes the life holy."[33] If we have true righteousness, we can enjoy that part of the kingdom that extends to the everlasting future where without clean hands and a pure heart, none shall see God. True obedience to the Law comes not from following external ritual. It has a far deeper meaning "affecting the relation of the heart to God."[34]

The impaired righteousness described in verse 19 only sets a person low on the scale in the kingdom of heaven. Here the scribes and Pharisees are deficient in true righteousness and face utter darkness and destruction. God expects genuine righteousness from His people. He will not endure a phony profession that does not live what it professes.

---

33 Barnes, 51.
34 Williams, 158.

The righteousness of the scribes and Pharisees was external. They worshipped with words and actions but not with the heart. God expects His people to have inward righteousness that comes from a pure heart. That is why He condemned lust as adultery (Matt. 5:28) and inspired John to condemn hate as murder (1 John 3:15). Not committing murder or adultery was insufficient if those evil passions reside in the heart.

It seems that God expects more of Christians, and that is so. Christians have light. They have a fuller righteousness taught in the New Testament and by the example of Christ's perfect life. Christians ought to live to a higher standard because it pleases God. Christ gives us righteousness and the power to be all that He expects of us. "Even the righteousness of God through faith in Jesus Christ for all those who believe; for there is no distinction" (Rom. 3:22). God reveals His righteousness in the Law, the Prophets, and the Writings "all bearing testimony to the great design of God and to the absolute necessity there was for the sacrifice and salvation which God has provided."[35] True righteousness that comes from clean hands and a pure heart exists only in those who are born again.

---

35 Adam Clarke, *Commentary on the Whole Bible*. (Tempe, AZ: The Crosswire Software and Bible Society, 1810/1825).

CHAPTER 3

THE OLD TESTAMENT

THIS CHAPTER IS NECESSARY BECAUSE there are many Christians who don't assign the same value to the Old Testament as they do the New Testament. That is folly. "We must view the New Testament as the next installment in the ongoing revelation and plan of God."[1] This chapter serves as a warning that such thinking is wrong, dangerous, and unscriptural.

Many good books exist that explain Old Testament structure, content, theology, and history. This book does not attempt to repeat what others have so ably written. Here the reader will find only a simple foundational framework necessary to illustrate the importance of the Old Testament as a vital part of the relationship between Law and Gospel.

The words of our Lord in Luke 24:44 indicate a threefold arrangement of the Old Testament. "Now He said to them, 'These are My words which I spoke to you while I was still with you, that all things which are written about Me in the Law of Moses and the Prophets and the Psalms must be fulfilled.'" The threefold arrangement is evident in the layout of the Masoretic Text (MT), which is different from the format in modern Bibles:[2]

---

1 Walter C. Kaiser, Jr., *Toward Rediscovering the Old Testament.* Paperback edition, 1991. (Grand Rapids, MI: Zondervan Publishing House, 1987), 99.
2 This is the most commonly accepted arrangement of the MT. More than sixty different arrangements are known for the Hebrew Scriptures. There are almost as many variations of order of books. The variations are due to limitations of writing materials available. There were too many books to put on a single scroll; owners arranged them in any order they desired. From Kaiser, 43-44.

- The Law of Moses is the Pentateuch.

- The Prophets in two groups

  - Former Prophets – Joshua, Judges, Samuel, and Kings (Samuel and Kings were not divided)

  - Latter Prophets – Isaiah, Jeremiah, Ezekiel, and the Twelve (the Twelve are the Minor Prophets)

- The Writings

  - Poetical Books – Psalms, Job, Proverbs

  - Five Rolls – Ruth, Song of Songs, Ecclesiastes, Lamentations, Esther

  - Historical Books – Daniel, Ezra-Nehemiah, Chronicles (Chronicles was not divided)

Only one Greek word, *nomos,* translates to the English word *law.* "*Nomos* became the established name for law as decreed by a state and set up as the standard for the administration of justice."[3] Specifically, *nomos* is the Law in the first five books of the Old Testament, the Torah. New Testament writers often refer to it as the Scriptures. Today Christians call it the Pentateuch or the Books of the Law, or occasionally by the Jewish name, the Torah.

The word *prophet* denotes one who speaks forth as a proclaimer of a divine message. In the Old Testament, they are the writers of the books of prophecy. Jesus sometimes included those books with the law. Christ is not just referring to the Torah, the first five books of Moses. Instead, He is speaking of the entire Old Testament. Many times Christ referred to the law and the prophets that support the authority and principles of the Old Testament (Matt. 7:12, 22:40, Luke 16:16). Jews read the law and the prophets in the synagogue (Acts 13:15).

---

3 William. E. Vine, *An Expository Dictionary of Old Testament Words.* Edited by F. F. Bruce. (Old Tappan, NJ: Fleming H. Revell Co., 1978), 653.

The Old Testament is divinely inspired. The authors knew they were writing the Word of God. "In the fourth year of Jehoiakim the son of Josiah, king of Judah, this word came to Jeremiah from the Lord, saying, "Take a scroll and write on it all the words which I have spoken to you concerning Israel and concerning Judah, and concerning all the nations, from the day I *first* spoke to you, from the days of Josiah, even to this day" (Jer. 36:1–2).

"They made their hearts *like* flint so that they could not hear the law and the words which the LORD of hosts had sent by His Spirit through the former prophets; therefore great wrath came from the LORD of hosts" (Zech. 7:12). Zechariah uses the phrase *law and the words* to indicate the Spirit of God inspired the words of the former prophets who ministered prior to his ministry.

The Old Testament claims to be the Word of God. More than 2,000 times[4] the reader will find statements such as "the Lord said," "thus says the Lord," or "the Lord commanded." The New Testament confirms the divine inspiration of the Old Testament. "Brethren, the Scripture had to be fulfilled, which the Holy Spirit foretold by the mouth of David concerning Judas, who became a guide to those who arrested Jesus" (Acts 1:16). This is a strong attestation to the divine inspiration of the book of Psalms. The Holy Spirit dictated the psalms to men. The early church recognized all the Old Testament was the Word of God and obeyed it. Old Testament prophecies are relevant to the completion of the gospel message and fulfillment of the plan of the ages.

---

4 The actual number depends upon who is doing the counting and the criteria they use. In most cases, quotes are easy to identify. Allusions are sometimes highly subjective. Nestle's Greek New Testament – 950 quotes and allusions, the United Bible Society's Greek Text – places the number at 2,500,; Wilhelm Dittmar identifies 1,640; and E. Huhn claims to have found 4,105 quotes and allusions. From Kaiser, 168. G. T. Manley maintains there are 1,603 quotations, references, and allusions that link the New Testament with the Old. G. T. Manley, "The New Bible Handbook," Chicago: The Intervarsity Christian Fellowship, 1949, 442-455, quoted in W. T. Purkiser, Demaray, C.E., Metz, Donald S., Stuneck, Maude A., *Exploring the Old Testament*, (Kansas City, MO: Beacon Hill Press of Kansas City, 1955), 48.

When the New Testament uses any term—law, Law of Moses, the prophets, or psalms—it gives legitimacy to the Old Testament as part of the eternal Word of God. When Christians read any of these terms in the New Testament that refer to the Old Testament, they can confidently believe both Testaments are from God. The fact that Jesus and other New Testament writers so often refer to the Old Testament assures the Christian of its validity.[5]

Two passages indicate the entire Old Testament is the law. Jesus says in John 10:34, "Has it not been written in your Law, 'I said, you are gods?'" He was quoting Psalm 82:6. Later Paul wrote in 1 Cor. 14:21, "In the Law it is written, 'By men of strange tongues and by the lips of strangers I will speak to this people, and even so they will not listen to Me,' says the Lord." He was quoting Isaiah 28:11–12. "The whole of Old Testament Scripture assumes the existence of the law, calls men back to the law, and threatens the penalties of the law for its violations."[6]

THE LORD JESUS CHRIST USED THE OLD TESTAMENT

The Gospels show Jesus makes at least forty-six separate direct quotes in the four Gospels and untold numbers of references to Old Testament history and people. Sixty-three times in the New Testament we find the phrase "it is written." Twenty-six of those are in the Gospels from the mouth of Christ. Each time He said, "It is written," He was quoting the Old Testament. Fourteen more times Jesus uses the word *written* to mean the Old Testament.

Much of what Christ said in the Gospels is an expansion and interpretation of the Mosaic Law. "The whole of the law then—not only the covenant but also the promises and threats, rules and regulations, sacrifices and ceremonies—finds its meaning in Christ who is its life, soul, spirit, substance, fulfillment, and goal."[7]

---

5 W. T. Purkiser, Demaray, C.E., Metz, Donald S., Stuneck, Maude A., *Exploring the Old Testament*, (Kansas City, MO: Beacon Hill Press of Kansas City, 1955), 48.
6 Alva J. McClain, *Law and Grace*. 1954. Reprint, (Chicago: Moody Press, 1967), 8.
7 I. John Hesselink, "Calvin's Concept and Use of the Law." Footnote 112 in *Five*

Five times Jesus referred to the Old Testament as the "commandment of God" or "commandment of an everlasting God." He declared the Old Testament would stand forever in Matthew 5:17–18.

Satan tempted Jesus at the beginning of His ministry. Three times Jesus thwarted Satan by quoting the law from the Old Testament book of Deuteronomy (Matt. 4:1–11, Mark 1:12–13, Luke 4:1–13).

When speaking of marriage, Jesus quoted Genesis 2:24. He answered the question of the Pharisees with this very telling phrase, "Have you not read that He who created *them* from the beginning made them male and female" (Matt. 19:4). There is little doubt He was speaking of the Creation story in Genesis.

Christ used the law to settle theological questions. When questioned by a lawyer, Jesus asked him, "What is written in the Law" (Luke 10:26)? On the occasion of the Pharisees challenging the disciples plucking grain on the Sabbath, Jesus asked, "Have you not read in the Law" (Matt. 12:5)?

Twice Jesus specifically mentioned he was quoting Isaiah, in Matthew 13:14 and Mark 7:6. Our Savior quoted Psalms at least ten times, more if including the parallel passages in the synoptics. On one occasion, when quoting Psalm 110, He even mentioned that David was the author (Matt. 22:44–45). He mentions Jonah twice (Matt. 12:39, 16:4), Noah (Matt. 24:37), and Daniel (Matt. 24:15). In three verses of Luke 4:25–27, Jesus mentions Elijah, Elisha, and Naaman the Syrian. Each time He mentions one of these Old Testament characters He is doing so in the context that they existed as revealed in the Old Testament. Jesus speaks of Old Testament events such as the Flood, the Exodus, Sodom and Gomorrah, and Jonah's fish as if they are authentic historical happenings. Jesus quotes or alludes to so many Old Testament passages that it is impossible to mention them all.

Views on Law and Gospel, by Stanley N. Gundry. ed. (Grand Rapids: Zondervan, 1996), 51.

Jesus and His disciples observed the Passover as commanded in the law (Matt. 26:17-19). Each time Jesus healed leprosy He instructed the cured person to "show yourself to the priest and present the offering that Moses commanded" (Matt. 8:4, Luke 17:14).

Christ taught the men on the Emmaus Road about Himself from the Old Testament. "Then beginning with Moses and with all the prophets, He explained to them the things concerning Himself in all the Scriptures" (Luke 24:27). All the Scriptures is "Law of Moses and the Prophets and the Psalms" (Luke 24:44). Christ spoke about how He is presented throughout the Old Testament. Certainly, He spoke of the sacrificial system, which speaks of His atonement, the many types, symbols, and allusions to His sufferings, death, and resurrection. No doubt, He also spoke of all the prophecies that foretold His appearing in "Law of Moses and the Prophets and the Psalms."

Take for example Jesus words, "In everything, therefore, treat people the same way you want them to treat you, for this is the Law and the Prophets" (Matthew 7:12). This is the Golden Rule, accepted by all as a worthy manner of living. It comes from Leviticus 19:18. Everyone accepts the Golden Rule even if it is rooted in the Old Testament.

Perhaps the greatest claim to the validity of the Old Testament is what Christ said when describing the witness of Himself found in Moses' words. "Do not think that I will accuse you before the Father; the one who accuses you is Moses, in whom you have set your hope. For if you believed Moses, you would believe Me, for he wrote about Me. But if you do not believe his writings, how will you believe My words" (John 5:45-47)? This is vital testimony on the authority of the Mosaic Law. Essentially, what He was saying is that what Moses wrote has the same value and importance as His words. "Christ is not opposed to the law, He is a fulfillment of its righteous demands."[8]

---

8 Harold Vaughn, An Unscriptural Division. *The Baptist Examiner.* June 11, 1998, 1, 8, 9.

Jesus used the Old Testament. He believed it, preached it, and practiced it. "To the Lord Jesus Christ the Old Testament was the Word of God; it was Scripture; it was something absolutely unique and apart; it had authority which nothing else has ever possessed nor can possess."[9] From His words, it is obvious that Jesus accepted the Old Testament Scriptures and regarded them as divine, authoritative, and infallible. Our Savior "accepts the Old Testament economy and its Scriptures as from God, as stamped with divine authority, as truly making known the divine mind and will."[10]

Christ obeyed and fulfilled Scripture. By His every word and deed, He endorsed the authority of the Old Testament. Men should accept it the same as He did, as divinely inspired and true.[11]

God spoke to the people of Israel, first by Moses, then by a succession of human prophets.

THE APOSTLES USED THE OLD TESTAMENT

Christ in the Gospels expanded and interpreted the Old Testament. The writers of the New Testament Epistles took it further. They not only preached and wrote about the Old Testament and the Law but also expanded and interpreted what Christ said about the Old Testament and the Law. The New Testament writers clearly understood that what they were writing about was the consummation of a redemptive history that began in the pages of the Old Testament.

Thirty-seven times the apostles use the phrase *it is written.* Eleven more times the apostles use the word *written.* In every instance, the context shows they are referring to the Old Testament.

---

9 D. Martyn Lloyd-Jones, *Studies in the Sermon on the Mount.* (Grand Rapids, MI: William B. Eerdmans Publishing Company, 1976), 163.

10 William Caven, The Testimony of Christ to the Old Testament, in *The Fundamentals*, vol. 1, R. A. Torrey, ed. reprint 1996, (Grand Rapids, MI: Baker Books, 1917), 209.

11 Taken from a lengthy quote by J. I. Packer in *The Fundamentals for the Twenty-First Century.* Mal Couch ed. (Grand Rapids, MI: Kregel Publications, 2000), 105.

The apostles followed our Savior's lead in their missionary and evangelistic efforts. They presented Christ in the synagogue using the Old Testament. The Gentile churches used the Old Testament to study. The noble Bereans used the Old Testament when they were "examining the Scriptures daily" (Acts 17:11).

Fifteen times in the Pastoral Epistles, Paul used the Greek word for teaching in reference to the Old Testament. On five of those occasions, he linked it with sound doctrine. Paul urged the church to use the Old Testament for teaching doctrine. The best information for some doctrines such as Creation and the fall of man are in the Old Testament. The New Testament only alludes to them. Christians cannot understand either without studying the Old Testament

In 2 Timothy 3:16–17 there are sound reasons for using the Old Testament: "Scripture is inspired by God and profitable for teaching, for reproof, for correction, for training in righteousness; so that the man of God may be adequate, equipped for every good work." Teaching means doctrinal truth. Reproof means to awaken men to their sin. Correction means to fix what is wrong by restoration to a right state before God. Instruction means to do what is necessary to keep things right by submitting to the rules of Christian growth. The Greek word translated *adequate (perfect* in the KJV) means mature or complete. The phrase *thoroughly furnished* means to be fully equipped with the right tools for the task God gives. The purpose of Scripture is to have a life that is full of good works that bring glory to God. The Scripture Paul is telling Timothy to study is the Old Testament. To be ready for "good works," Christians must study both Testaments, all the Scriptures.

After his arrest in Jerusalem, Paul referred to the Old Testament in his defense: "But this I admit to you, that according to the Way which they call a sect I do serve the God of our fathers, believing everything that is in accordance with the Law and that is written in the Prophets" (Acts 24:14). In his epistle to the Romans, Paul said, "For whatever was written in earlier times was written for our instruction, so that through perseverance and the encouragement of the Scriptures we might have hope" (Rom. 15:4). Things "written in earlier times" were the Old Testament books, written for the instruction of Christians.

Paul warned the Corinthian church to avoid making the same mistakes of disobedience that Israel did. After listing some of their sins, he reminded them: "Now these things happened to them as an example, and they were written for our instruction, upon whom the ends of the ages have come" (1 Cor. 10:11). The problems of Israel revealed in the Old Testament are there to be an example of correct living for Christians.

At the time Peter penned, "for no prophecy was ever made by an act of human will, but men moved by the Holy Spirit spoke from God" (2 Pet. 1:21), a third of the New Testament was yet to be written. In effect, there was no New Testament, just some important letters from key apostles. Peter was speaking of the Old Testament, pointing out to his readers that Old Testament prophecy is a sure evidence of divine revelation. "The meaning of the Apostle appears to be this: The law and the prophets have spoken concerning Jesus Christ."[12] In that passage, Peter reminded them of the Mount of Transfiguration that he, James, and John experienced. He told his readers they "have also a more sure word of prophecy; whereunto ye do well that ye take heed" (2 Pet. 1:19, KJV). The "more sure word of prophecy" is the Old Testament, and it is more valuable to believers than the events on the mountain.

The words *Scripture* or *Scriptures* appear fifty-three times in the New Testament. Each and every time, the context indicates the need to study the Old Testament. In 2 Timothy 3:16 the Greek word translated "scripture" is *graphe*. It always refers to the canon of Scripture throughout the Bible. It is associated with New Testament writings. Paul used that same word, *graphe*, in 1 Timothy 5:18. "For the Scripture says, 'You shall not muzzle the ox while he is threshing,' and 'The laborer is worthy of his wages.'" In that verse, Paul is quoting both

---

12 Commentary on 2 Peter 1:19. Adam Clarke, *Commentary on the Whole Bible.* (Tempe, AZ The Crosswire Software and Bible Society, 1810/1825).

Testaments. The first is Deuteronomy 25:4. "You shall not muzzle the ox while he is threshing." The second is the words of Christ in Luke 10:7. "Stay in that house, eating and drinking what they give you; for the laborer is worthy of his wages. Do not keep moving from house to house." In this one verse, Paul declared both Testaments have equal standing as Scripture!

"Then Philip opened his mouth, and beginning from this Scripture he preached Jesus to him" (Acts 8:35). Philip upon joining up with the Ethiopian eunuch preached from Isaiah 53. The Ethiopian received salvation from hearing the Word of God expounded from the Old Testament!

Writing of our beloved brother Paul, Peter says, "As also in all *his* letters, speaking in them of these things, in which are some things hard to understand, which the untaught and unstable distort, as *they do* also the rest of the Scriptures, to their own destruction." Peter uses the word *graphe* for "Scriptures" (2 Peter 3:16). In effect, Peter equated Paul's writings with the "other Scriptures," the Old Testament.

In Romans 7:22 Paul says, "For I joyfully concur with the law of God in the inner man." The Greek word translated as "law" refers to the Mosaic Law. The Greek word for "delight" appears only here in the New Testament. It is a strong word and indicates intellectual and emotional consent to the law. It expresses both the state of mind and the heart of Paul. He echoes David, "O how I love Your law! It is my meditation all the day" (Ps. 119:97). It is inconceivable that Paul, a converted Pharisee who knew the Mosaic Law better than most men, would write such a statement if he thought the law was invalid in the Church Age. As the author of thirteen epistles where he expounded on the grace and mercy of the Savior, he could only make such a statement if it were true. The sense is that Paul is fully satisfied and pleased with all the Old Testament communications and divine instructions passed from God to man.

Paul followed Christ's example in theological discussion by referring to the law. In defense of a paid ministry, he quoted a passage from Deuteronomy 25:4, declaring, "For it is written in the Law of Moses" (1 Cor. 9:9).

Peter, James, John, Jude, and Paul used more than 250 direct quotations from the Old Testament. Additionally, there are a vast number of references and allusions that draw on the terminology and mode of thought and expression be found in the Hebrew Scriptures.

CHRISTIANS MUST USE THE OLD TESTAMENT

Far too many Christians look at the Old Testament and see nothing but Psalms, Proverbs, and a few children's Bible stories. Ken Casillas expresses concern that the average Christian is not doing much with the Old Testament. He writes, "God's revelation in the Old Testament is often ignored, contributing to the unholiness of many who profess Christ."[13] This is a great tragedy, for everything in the Word of God is valid for all men in any age. "Now these things happened to them as an example, and they were written for our instruction, upon whom the ends of the ages have come" (1 Cor. 10:11).

Isaiah wrote concerning the Word of God, "The grass withers, the flower fades, but the word of our God stands forever" (Isaiah 40:8). Peter quoted him, "for you have been born again not of seed which is perishable but imperishable, *that is*, through the living and enduring Word of God. For, 'all flesh is like grass, and all its glory like the flower of grass. The grass withers, and the flower falls off, but the word of the Lord endures forever.' And this is the word which was preached to you" (1 Pet. 1:23–25). When Peter quoted Isaiah, much of the New Testament was unwritten. Peter was endorsing Isaiah's words concerning the value and usefulness of the Old Testament for Christians.

---

13 Ken Casillas, *The Law and the Christian*. (Greenville, SC: Bob Jones University Press, 2007), 25.

Christians who refuse to use the Old Testament are sinning. The Holy Spirit directed the writing of both Testaments, all sixty-six books. The two Testaments combine to make the whole Bible. Jesus' approach to the Old Testament seems to say, "All this is of God and I am come to carry it out and to fulfill it."[14] Men who question the authority of the Old Testament are questioning the authority of God. God the Father is predominant in the Old Testament. Jesus said in John 10:30, "I and My Father are One." We cannot separate and elevate any part of the Triune Godhead above another. The Triune Godhead wrote both Testaments. Thus, we cannot separate and elevate one Testament over the other.

More than three-fourths of the Bible is in the Old Testament. Excluding any part of the Old Testament will affect nearly every area of theology. "By any fair reckoning, it is impossible to teach the 'whole counsel of God' without deeply involving oneself in the details of Old Testament life and thought."[15]

If Christians were to disregard the law, Old Testament passages such as, "Open my eyes, that I may behold wonderful things from Your law" (Ps. 119:18) would be irrelevant. That places men in the dangerous position of picking and choosing which portions of Scripture are valid. How can the created being select which of the Creator's words have value? That is little more than negotiating with God, and worse it is a foolish attempt to make ourselves like God.

The Old Testament has very clear injunctions against divination, magicians, necromancy, soothsayers, sorcery, and witchcraft. These sins are equally reprehensible in the New Testament. The apostles acted swiftly when they encountered them.[16] No true believer questions those portions of the law that condemn occult activities in the age of grace. The Old Testament actively insists on holiness and justice in every relationship men can have, with God and with other men.

---

14 Lloyd-Jones, 164.
15 Kaiser, 17.
16 Acts 8:11–24, 13:6–11, 16:16–18

God's people must not reject or take lightly any portion of the Old Testament. It was important to our Lord, it is important to us.

- Do not dilute any part of the Creation with modern science.

- Do not question the Exodus because archaeologists have not found the trail.

- Do not question the existence of King David just because archaeologists have not found his name on stone carvings in Jerusalem.

- Do not doubt the virgin birth simply because linguists argue over the meaning of the Hebrew word translated *virgin* in Isaiah 7:14.

- Do not treat Psalms, Proverbs, and the Prophets as nothing more than poetry by those who wrote inspiring words about life and the human condition.

The Belgic Confession states, "We still use the testimonies taken out of the law and the prophets, to confirm us in the doctrine of the Gospel, and to regulate our life in all honesty to the glory of God, according to his will."[17] Those words point to a practical, sensible position for believers to take concerning the importance of the Law in Christian living.

CHRIST IS IN THE OLD TESTAMENT

Fifteen[18] times in the New Testament are quotes or references to Deuteronomy 18:15–19 that point to Christ as the Messiah to come. Several of those passages show the penalty for disobeying the law was the same as the penalty for disobeying Christ.

[15]The Lord your God will raise up for you a prophet like me from among you, from your countrymen, you shall listen

---

17 Quoted by William A. VanGemeren. A Response to Greg L. Bahnsen, *The Theonomic Reformed Approach to Law and Gospel.* in Gundry, Stanley N. ed. *Five Views of Law and the Gospel,* (Grand Rapids: Zondervan, 1996), 146.

18 Matthew 21:11, Luke 2:25–34, 7:16, 24:19, John 1:21, 1:25, 4:19, 4:25, 8:28, 12:49, 12:50, 17:8, Acts 3:22, 3:23, 7:37

to him. ¹⁶This is according to all that you asked of the Lord your God in Horeb on the day of the assembly, saying, "Let me not hear again the voice of the Lord my God, let me not see this great fire anymore, or I will die."

¹⁷The Lord said to me, "They have spoken well. ¹⁸I will raise up a prophet from among their countrymen like you, and I will put My words in his mouth, and he shall speak to them all that I command him. ¹⁹It shall come about that whoever will not listen to My words which he shall speak in My name, I Myself will require *it* of him."

In Deuteronomy 18:16, Moses is referring to the events surrounding the giving of the tables of stone written on by the hand of God. They went to the mountain, heard the voice of God, were afraid, and asked that God would use a man to speak to them (Deut. 5:24–28, Heb. 12:19–20). God acknowledged they were correct and that they spoke well. Their request showed true fear and respect for the holy things of God. At Sinai, they begged Moses to bring them God's Word. Ultimately, God gave them their request in the most wonderful way possible. He sent His only Son as a man to bring them the Word. Christ is a true man, but also the Prophet, Son of God. The Prophet will speak the words of God. Every word from Jesus is from God the Father.

Moses writes that God will raise up a Prophet who is a man. This is the clearest promise of our Lord in all the Law of Moses. John the Baptist refers to this passage when he speaks of the humanity of Christ. The people asked John the Baptist if he were the Prophet of whom Moses spoke. He replied that he was not; instead he was the forerunner of the Prophet who was coming after him (John 1:19–27). The people remembered this promise when they said about Jesus, "This is truly the Prophet who is to come into the world" (John 6:14).

The word translated *Prophet* Deuteronomy 18:15–19 is singular. It can only mean one person, the Lord Jesus Christ, and we can be certain that Moses intended this as a promise of the coming of the Messiah.

No Old Testament prophet qualified to be a Prophet with the same authority and connection with God as Moses. The prophet Moses is speaking of is the Messiah, first spoken of in the Garden after the fall (Gen. 3:15). Peter quoted Moses when he preached in the temple, "Moses said, 'The Lord God will raise up for you a prophet like me from your brethren; to Him you shall give heed to everything He says to you. And it will be that every soul that does not heed that prophet shall be utterly destroyed from among the people'" (Acts 3:22–23). Stephen spoke of this Prophet that Moses foretold in the sermon that led to his martyrdom (Acts 7:37).

Contemporaries of Jesus knew this prophecy, "Philip found Nathanael and said to him, 'We have found Him of whom Moses in the Law and *also* the Prophets wrote—Jesus of Nazareth, the son of Joseph'" (John 1:45).

God himself applied this to our Lord Jesus on the Mount of Transfiguration, "For when He received honor and glory from God the Father, such an utterance as this was made to Him by the Majestic Glory, 'This is My beloved Son with whom I am well-pleased'" (2 Pet. 1:17). Moses told them to listen to the future Prophet. On the Mount, Moses and Elijah stood by in agreement.

Peter preached Moses' words about the Prophet as truth, "Moses said, 'The Lord God will raise up for you a prophet like me from your brethren; to Him you shall give heed to everything He says to you'" (Acts 3:22).

The New Testament writers repeated and ratified the sentence Moses passed on those that heard and rejected this Prophet. "For if those did not escape when they refused him who warned *them* on earth, much less *will* we *escape* who turn away from Him who *warns* from heaven" (Heb. 12:25).

Jesus verified the warning that Moses wrote about those who would not listen to the prophet. "He who believes in the Son has eternal life; but he who does not obey the Son will not see life, but the wrath of God abides on him" (John 3:36).

More than one hundred prophecies foretell Jesus' birth, life, ministry, miracles, death, resurrection, and coming glory. From Zechariah 13:7, "Strike the Shepherd that the sheep may be scattered" becomes history in Matthew 26:31 when the disciples abandon Jesus. Psalm 41:9 predicts His betrayal by Judas.

Jesus quotes Psalm 35:19 and 69:4 when describing the unending malevolence of the opposition He faced from the religious leaders: "But *they have done this* to fulfill the word that is written in their Law, 'They hated Me without a cause'" (John 15:25).

Of course, there are more, many more references to Christ in "the law, the prophets, and the writings." Jesus, who we read about in the New Testament, is the Messiah of Israel and the hope of the nations predicted in the Old Testament. The life on earth of the Lord Jesus Christ is throughout the Old Testament. "But all this has taken place to fulfill the Scriptures of the prophets" (Matt. 26:56).

Finally, there are the words of our Lord: "You search the Scriptures because you think that in them you have eternal life; it is these that testify about Me" (John 5:39). With this sentence, the Lord Jesus declares Himself the central theme and subject of all written revelation in the Old Testament. That ought to settle it for all men.

CHAPTER 4

THE CHRISTIAN'S RELATIONSHIP TO THE LAW

BOTH LAW IN THE OLD Testament and Gospel of the New Testament are the Word of God, pertain to all men, and both ought to be preached. The only difference between the two is the Law condemns and the Gospel saves. "For the Law brings about wrath" (Rom. 4:15) that condemns sinful men. "For God did not send his Son into the world to condemn the world, but in order that the world might be saved through him" (John 3:17, ESV). "It is vitally important that we learn to recognize the difference between these two doctrines."[1]

The first thing to understand when discussing a distinction between two things is there are two things, not one. The gospel is not a law. The God-given law has not changed since Moses. The gospel of Christ is not something superior to the law Moses received. In fulfilling the Law, Christ improved it.

Martin Luther wrote: "Let every Christian learn diligently to distinguish between the Law and the Gospel."[2] The distinction is not a theory but is the heart of the Christian faith. Thomas K. Johnson elaborates on Luther's words, writing of the biblical message "as always having

---

1 Rick Ritchie, "What is This Law and Gospel Thing?" *Modern Reformation*, March/April 1993, 7-11.
2 Martin Luther, *Luther's Works*, ed. and trans. Jaroslav Pelikan, assoc. ed. Walter A Hansen, vol. 26: Lectures on Galatians, 1535 (St. Louis: Concordia Publishing House, 1963), 120.

two distinct but inseparable dimensions: command and promise, Law and Gospel."[3]

The Law condemns. That was not what Christ came to do. He did not bring more law. He spoke about law, but He did not give a law. He brought a Gospel of grace and mercy and peace. In doing so, He fulfilled the Law. "Men must be made to understand the God of the New Testament is the same as He was in Old Testament times. He has not changed."[4] To separate His law from grace is to pervert the Bible and throw the door open for unabashed sin in the house of God.

John Wesley explains the law is useful "both to convince unbelievers, and to guide believers in all holiness. We grant the whole Mosaic Law is good, answers excellent purposes, if a man uses it in a proper manner. Even the ceremonial is good, as it points to Christ; and the moral law is holy, just, and good, on its own nature; and of admirable use both to convince unbelievers, and to guide believers in all holiness."[5] It is essential that men know enough about the structure of the law so they can "use it lawfully" without distortion, confusion, or heresy.

ROMANS 3:31

Paul, speaking of justification, wrote: "Do we then nullify the Law through faith? May it never be! On the contrary, we establish the Law" (Rom. 3: 31). Paul asks whether the doctrine of justification cancels' the law. The phrase "May it never be!" has the idea of "far from it," or "by no means." Paul answers his own question with an emphatic NO! He is forcefully declaring it does not. It does just the opposite. Far from it, Paul states, "we establish the law" to show its excellence and never-changing obligations. Christians recognize the law so it can lead

---

3 Thomas K. Johnson, Law and Gospel. *Evangelical Review of Theology*, vol. 36, no. 2, April 2012, 151.

4 Harold Vaughn, An Unscriptural Division. *The Baptist Examiner.* June 11, 1998, 1, 8, 9.

5 Comments on 1 Timothy 1:8. John Wesley, *John Wesley's Notes on the Bible.* Based on the electronic edition by Sulu Kelley and Bill Brown, (Tempe, AZ: The Crosswire Software and Bible Society).

men to persevere with sincerity in their attempts to be successfully obedient to God who created the law.

Both uses of the word "law" in Romans 3:31 mean the whole of the Mosaic Law, including its rites and ceremonies. The word *establish* is variously translated uphold, confirm, or to cause to stand. The word translated as *faith* denotes the persuasion and moral conviction of the truthfulness of God, especially reliance upon Christ for salvation. Schofield writes, "The sinner establishes the law in its right use and honor by confessing his guilt, and acknowledging that by it he is justly condemned. Christ, on the sinner's behalf, establishes the law by enduring its penalty, which is death."[6] The fact that God saves sinners through faith in Christ does not devalue the importance and authority of His law as an expression of His will. Never forget, God first showed the way of saving sinners in the Old Testament. In the Book of Acts, the apostles preached salvation by faith using the Law, the Writings, and the Prophets.

DIVISIONS OF THE LAW

Probably the most common view of the Mosaic Law separates it into three divisions: moral, ceremonial, and judicial (civil). The ceremonial law regulated worship practices. The judicial law covered government and the courts. Both belonged to the Jewish people and only to them until the coming of the Messiah. The moral law served as the ruler of conscience and life. It introduced the knowledge of sin into every conscience "for through the Law *comes* the knowledge of sin" (Rom. 3:20). Typically, adherents of this view maintain only the moral law is applicable in the Church Age.

There are contrary opinions. G. J. Wenham calls it an arbitrary distinction, pointing to "the arrangement of the material in Leviticus. Love of neighbor immediately precedes a prohibition on mixed

---

6 Commentary on Romans 3:31. C.I. Schofield, *Scofield Reference Notes* 1917 edition, based on the version at http://bible.crosswalk.com/ with formatting changes and corrections. (Tempe, AZ: The Crosswire Software and Bible Society).

breeding; the holiness motto comes just before the law on executing unruly children (Lev. 19:18–19; 20:7–9)."[7] In many instances, it is impossible to determine any difference between moral and judicial law. Attempts to separate the two create a confusing patchwork of divisions of the Word of God, one verse moral, the next verse judicial, and the verse after that difficult to quantify.

Another position looks to the words of Christ: "For verily I say unto you, Till heaven and earth pass, one jot or one tittle shall in no wise pass from the Law, till all be fulfilled" (Matt 5:18, KJV). Adherents of that position argue that all the law, including ceremonial and judicial, is valid in the Church Age, though they struggle with the sacrificial rites. Other scholars hold widely varying stances on the divisions of the law. Denominational positions further confuse the landscape. Supporters of each position strengthen their position with a carefully selected list of verses. As so often is the case with theological and doctrinal differences, the answer is, as usual, somewhere in the middle of each humanly declared position.

George B. Stevens asks if Jesus specified a distinction between the ceremonial and moral parts of the law. He said, "If He did not, how are they to be distinguished? It is common to make a distinction between the ceremonial and the moral divisions of the law and to suppose that, while the former are done away, the latter are still binding upon Christians."[8] Stevens is quick to declare, and correctly, there is no such distinction evident in either Testament. The biblicist view is that nowhere in the Bible can anyone find a three-part division of the Mosaic Law. There is nothing written in any Jewish literature that separates the law into three parts. The Jews consider all of the law to be a single entity without division.

---

7 G. J. Wenhan, *The Book of Leviticus*, NICOT (Grand Rapids: Erdmans, 1979), 34 in Wayne G. Strickland. The Inauguration of the Law of Christ with the Gospel of Christ: A Dispensational View, in Five Views on Law and Gospel, by Stanley N. Gundry. ed. (Grand Rapids: Zondervan, 1996), 262.

8 George B. Stevens, Gospel and Law in the Teaching of Jesus Christ. *Searching Together*, Spring-Autumn 1992, 9-16.

No one of orthodox thinking would attempt to divide the Sermon on the Mount into parts as some do the law. Yet, it contains moral, judicial, and ceremonial instructions. The moral law is obvious throughout in commandments for believers to obey. Matthew 5:23–24 speaks of bringing gifts to the altar. This is the language of the sacrificial system. Note also Matthew 5:21 where Jesus says, "Whoever commits murder shall be liable to the court." The court is the Sanhedrin who tried lawbreakers.

When Paul wrote of "the Law of commandments *contained* in ordinances" (Eph. 2:15), he was referring to the whole law. In Scripture, it is the law of God, Law of Moses, or just Law. From Sinai until the resurrection of Christ, there was a Law. After the resurrection, there is still a Law. The difference is that Christ fulfilled the Law. It remains in effect and will always be in effect in its fulfilled state.

The Gospel reveals and explains the types, shadows, and prophecies contained in the Law. We can confidently rely on the fulfillment of every detail of His preordained plan of the ages. The Gospel does not repeal any part of the Law, but fulfills all of it, thus more fully and completely establishes all of it.

The Moral Instructions of the Law Have Priority

The Law is a whole, but the mind of God has a greater interest in the observance of the moral and ethical commands in the law that encourages obedience. "Samuel said, 'Has the Lord as much delight in burnt offerings and sacrifices as in obeying the voice of the Lord? Behold, to obey is better than sacrifice, *and* to heed than the fat of rams'" (1 Sam. 15:22). Samuel pointedly told Saul that God preferred a pure and obedient heart attitude instead of an empty religious ceremony.[9]

Kaiser explains: "The moral law of God took precedence over the civil and ceremonial laws in that it was based on the character of

---

9 See also Isaiah 1:11–17, Jeremiah 7:21–23, and Micah 6:8.

God."[10] It is unquestionably true that the character of God is love and holiness. For that reason, love and holiness can serve as a summary of what the law demands. The remainder of the law—the rites, the ceremonies, and the civil—functioned as types and shadows to point to the coming of Christ.

Nowhere is the priority of obedience over ceremony more clear than the heartfelt prayer of David confessing his sin: "For You do not delight in sacrifice, otherwise I would give it; You are not pleased with burnt offering. The sacrifices of God are a broken spirit; a broken and a contrite heart, O God, You will not despise" (Ps. 51:16–17).

One Law

Despite the primacy of the moral aspects of the law, do not separate it out as more important in the Church Age. "This law is one law—an indivisible unity. While it is unquestionably true that at least three elements appear within this law, it is wrong to divide it into three laws."[11] The distinctions between the ritualistic, civil, and moral law is modern."[12] It is an artificial construct to make for easy understanding or to support a system of theology. That is all. Nothing more. Scripture does not support dividing the law into the three parts, and doing so creates more problems than it solves.

THE LAW IS ETERNAL

Scripture foretells the end of the world. "Then I saw a new heaven and a new earth; for the first heaven and the first earth passed away, and there is no longer *any* sea" (Revelation 21:1). Until that momentous day, nearly every other reference to the heavens and the earth in the

---

10 Walter C. Kaiser, Jr., *The Law as God's Gracious Guidance for the Promotion of Holiness* in Gundry, Stanley N. ed. *Five Views of Law and the Gospel*, (Grand Rapids: Zondervan, 1996), 190.

11 Alva J. McClain, *Law and Grace.* 1954. Reprint, (Chicago: Moody Press, 1967), 8.

12 H. A..W. Meyer, Matthew: Commentary on the New Testament (New York: Funk and Wagnals, 1884. Quoted in McClain, Alva J. *Law and Grace.* 1954. Reprint, (Chicago: Moody Press, 1967), 9.

Word of God is that of stability. The universe is here to stay, no matter what men may do or what environmentalists claim, until God replaces it with the New Jerusalem.

> "He set the earth on its foundations, so that it should never be moved" (Ps. 104:5, ESV).

> "Your faithfulness endures to all generations; you have established the earth, and it stands fast" (Ps. 119:90, ESV).

> "A generation goes and a generation comes, But the earth remains forever" (Eccles. 1:4).

In three identical passages, the Gospel writers quote Jesus, "Heaven and earth will pass away, but My words will not pass away" (Matt. 24:35, Mark 13:31, Luke 21:33). Though Jesus was speaking of the fall of Jerusalem, "All this vast creation, earth, and stars will disappear in their turn, but these sayings of mine, which predict their future passing away into nothingness, will outlive both earth and heaven."[13]

Jesus says the Law will not pass away. In Matthew 5:18 Jesus said, "For truly I say to you, until heaven and earth pass away, not the smallest letter or stroke shall pass from the Law until all is accomplished." The parallel passage in Luke 16:17 provides clarity, "But it is easier for heaven and earth to pass away than for one stroke of a letter of the Law to fail." Jesus is asserting the perpetuity of the Law in this age. His words indicate that even if it were possible for heaven and earth to pass away, the Law will still stand. His coming did not abolish or replace the Law. There will always be the Law. In essence, Jesus is saying in Matthew 5:18, It is and shall be so, I, the *Amen*, the faithful Witness, solemnly declare that until time shall be no more, and there is a new heaven and a new earth; only then at the end of time will the Law be no more.

---

13 H. D. M. Spence, St. Luke in the Pulpit Commentary, ed. H.D.M. Spence & Joseph Exell. (New York: Funk & Wagnalls, 1913), 187.

In all the operations of human history, from Creation until now, this very moment, God is fulfilling the Scripture. That includes every bit of the Old Testament: the Law, the Prophets, and the Writings. That includes every event in history since the death and resurrection of Christ. It also includes the future events that Christ will fulfill at the Second Advent.

Since God's plan of eternity centers on Christ fulfilling the Law, then it must remain in effect as long as the heavens and the earth exist. Not one bit of the Law will ever pass away in this age. "Though all earth and hell should join together to hinder the accomplishment of the great designs of the Most High, yet it shall all be in vain—even the sense of a single letter shall not be lost. The words of God, which point out his designs, are as unchangeable as His nature itself."[14] God's laws will continue: "They stand this day according to Your ordinances" (Ps. 119:91).

The law of God is the eternal and unchangeable foundation of God's moral government. It is holy, just, and good. The inability of fallen man, to fulfill its precepts arises entirely from the pervasiveness of sin. The Lord Jesus Christ is the Mediator who will deliver repentant men and restore them to unfeigned obedience to the holy Law. That is the one great purpose of the Gospel and of the means of grace connected with the Gospel.

The law is the Book of the Ages. "Forever, O Lord, Your word is settled in heaven" (Ps. 119:89). "Of old I have known from Your testimonies that You have founded them forever" (Ps. 119:152). In both these verses the Hebrew word translated *forever* means everlasting, eternal, perpetual. Nothing that can happen in later human history, especially in biblical scholarship, will change the meaning of *forever*. This is not just an Old Testament idea. Matthew, Mark, and Luke record Jesus saying, "Heaven and earth will pass away, but My words will not pass away"

---

14 Commentary on Matthew 5:18. Adam Clarke, *Commentary on the Whole Bible.* (Tempe, AZ: The Crosswire Software and Bible Society, 1810/1825).

(Matt. 24:35, Mark 13:31, Luke 21:33). Peter makes a similar statement, "But the word of the Lord endures forever. And this is the word which was preached to you" (1 Pet. 1:25). The elimination of its smallest letter is no more likely than the obliteration of the universe—all of creation.

THE LAW, THE GOSPEL, THE ENTIRE WORD OF GOD

The whole Bible, both Testaments, is the Book of the Ages. It is divinely inspired food for the soul. Its precepts are written in the heart where it furnishes a light and is loved by the saints. It is mighty in its influence. It is a devouring flame, a crushing hammer, a life-giving force, a saving power, a defensive weapon, and a probing instrument. The law of God is a blessing to those who reverence it for it purifies the life.

"The law has never served any purpose for justification; but it had an enormous contribution to make in the area of sanctification and living life to the fullest as God had intended for his people to live."[15] The law had a future purpose to authenticate the divinity of Christ, to give hope to men, to relate human experience as a warning, and for reading in the congregation. It is the standard of faith and duty. Its words are sacred, and studying them is essential. It is absolutely trustworthy and profitable for instruction. Ignorance of it is perilous. Its message is for all men. It is pure, showing the perfection of the divine. God's people must keep it in their heart. It is impartial and, with its fulfillment by Christ, perpetual.

Diminishing the status and role of the Old Testament and the Mosaic Law is folly and guarantees a weaker, less knowledgeable Christian walk. Believers must understand that everything in the New Testament explains the inner meaning of the Law and brings forth its living spirit. The law of God is "holy, righteous, and good."

---

15 Walter C. Kaiser, response to Douglas J. Moo in *The Law of Christ as the Fulfillment of the Law of Moses: A Modified Lutheran View* in Gundry, Stanley N. ed. *Five Views of Law and the Gospel,* (Grand Rapids: Zondervan, 1996), 397.

The violation of it is unspeakably wicked. Men cannot violate the law and remain obedient to God.

As the prophets and priests were responsible for the ministry of the Old Testament, the apostles were responsible for the delivery of the New Testament. No Jew was exempt from the letter of the law found in the Old Testament. That was the way God chose for Jews to express their worship, their mind, and their heart to Him. The Gospel, which fulfilled the Law, meant the writers of the New Testament were not ministers of the letter (every jot and title) but of the spirit of the Gospel of Christ. In Christianity, the spirit (our heart attitude) is everything; the letter is a secondary consideration. "God is spirit, and those who worship Him must worship in spirit and truth" (John 4:24).

Moses, even though called the lawgiver, did not create the law that bears his name. God created the law and gave the law to Israel to instruct them in holiness. Christians would do well to remember the law comes from the mouth of God. "With my lips I have told of all the ordinances of Your mouth" (Ps. 119:13). God's people must avoid the tendency to assign the law to Moses rather than its divine source.

We must remember Paul's warning to Titus: "But avoid foolish controversies and genealogies and strife and disputes about the Law, for they are unprofitable and worthless" (Titus 3:9). He gave Timothy a similar warning: "But refuse foolish and ignorant speculations, knowing that they produce quarrels" (2 Tim. 2:23, ESV). Paul forbids them to engage in controversy over the law because it is a waste of time. Do not get involved in worldly arguments on such details that appeal to men in an effort to make themselves look wise.

Peter refers to passages from the law when he writes, "Because it is written, 'You shall be holy, for I am holy'" (1 Pet. 1:16). He was quoting from Leviticus 11:44–45, 19:2, and 20:7. Certainly, those words of the law are applicable to all Christians, or Peter wouldn't have cited them as instructions for his readers to be obedient children. Peter makes God's holiness, first revealed in the law, the standard of sanctification and requires Christians to follow it. The holiness required in Peter's quotes from the Old Testament is the same holiness that God expects from Church Age Christians.

FULFILLMENT OF PROPHECY BY CHRIST

Christians must be aware that more than one hundred times specific Old Testament prophecies achieve fulfillment in the life of Jesus Christ. The Old Testament prophecies foretold the coming of Christ's birth, life, death, and resurrection. If the Old Testament was no longer valid, then the very foundation of the New Testament becomes questionable. In Matthew 12:17–21, Jesus quoted Isaiah 42:1–3 concerning His earthly ministry, saying in verse 17, "*This was* to fulfill what was spoken through Isaiah the prophet." All that Jesus did on earth has its roots in the Old Testament.

Predictions concerning the Lord Jesus Christ are not limited to the seventeen books of prophecy. According to the words of our Lord, the message of hope for humanity is throughout the Old Testament. "Now He said to them, These are My words which I spoke to you while I was still with you, that all things which are written about Me in the Law of Moses and the Prophets and the Psalms must be fulfilled" (Luke 24:44).

Jesus continued in verse 45, "Then He opened their minds to understand the Scriptures." The "Scriptures" are the Old Testament. Jesus taught from the Old Testament, the apostles preached from the Old Testament, and the Bereans studied from the Old Testament. Believers today ought to follow that example and not neglect to use the very efficacious Old Testament for teaching, preaching, and study.

The statement found in Psalm 69:21, "They also gave me gall for my food, and for my thirst they gave me vinegar to drink," came to fulfillment on the cross. This verse specifically foreshadows how Jesus would receive gall and vinegar at his crucifixion. First, His executioners offered Him wine mixed with gall to help alleviate pain. Jesus rejected the painkiller (Matt. 27:32–34), choosing instead to drink the full cup of suffering his Father had given him (John 18:11). Later, just before he died, Jesus cried out in thirst and was given wine vinegar to drink (John 19:28–30). Jesus was well aware of the Messianic prophecies, and he fulfilled each one—even one as specific as this one—involving gall and vinegar—buried there in the book of Psalms.

The words of Peter are just as applicable today as they were in his sermon on the Temple portico: "But the things which God announced beforehand by the mouth of all the prophets, that His Christ would suffer, He has thus fulfilled" (Acts 3:18). The prophets declared the coming of the Lord Jesus Christ, some in very explicit words, others by symbols and types. The entire Old Testament religious system signified the coming of Christ and His work on Calvary. Thus, whether they understood it or not, everyone who prophesied, preached, or ministered in the temple had to have declared Him also.

THE COMMANDMENTS OF THE LAW TO BE KEPT

God's plan in giving His law to the Jews was to lead them to eternal life. Since all the law refers to Christ, and He became the end of the law to justify all men who chose to believe on Him. Obedience naturally follows belief, so keeping the commandments accomplishes that which the law required. Speaking to the rich young ruler, Jesus said, "Why are you asking Me about what is good? There is *only* One who is good; but if you wish to enter into life, keep the commandments" (Matt. 19:17). Some will say Jesus spoke these words in the Old Testament economy, so they do not apply in the Church Age. The phrase "keep the commandments" is a command that believers must obey in this age, just as Jesus expected the rich young ruler to obey. If we believe in the Lord Jesus Christ, then true faith requires us to love and obey God's law by keeping the commandments.

"By this we know that we love the children of God, when we love God and observe His commandments. For this is the love of God, that we keep His commandments; and His commandments are not burdensome" (1 John 5:2–3). When John wrote these words, there was no New Testament canon. The church read and obeyed the Old Testament. Our love to God is tested by whether we are "keeping His commandments." The only evidence of our love of God is that we keep His commandments.

The moral instruction of the Mosaic Law continues to be a standard of sanctification for Christians who read and obey the New Testament. "We must presume that every Old Testament commandment, even the least, continues to bind us unless teaching from Christ or the apostles elsewhere qualifies or alters that presumption."[16]

Paul clearly praises the law. "So then, the Law is holy, and the commandment is holy and righteous and good" (Rom. 7:12). It makes good sense that something that is holy, righteous, and good (something holy, righteous, and good can only come from God) would be a useful aid to the gospel and in living a life of faith and obedience.

There are a seemingly inexhaustible number of biblical examples to illustrate how the commands and instructions in the Mosaic Law have applicability to Christians living under grace. The rabbis knew the heart of the law was not circumcision, Sabbath keeping, or dietary regulations, but Deuteronomy 6:4–5, "Hear, O Israel! The Lord is our God, the Lord is one! You shall love the Lord your God with all your heart and with all your soul and with all your might." This is unquestionably true in the Church Age.

Paul repeats four of the Ten Commandments in Romans 13:8–10, "Owe nothing to anyone except to love one another; for he who loves his neighbor has fulfilled *the* law. For this, "You shall not commit adultery, You shall not murder, You shall not steal, You shall not covet," and if there is any other commandment, it is summed up in this saying, "You shall love your neighbor as yourself." Love does no wrong

---

16 Greg L. Bahnsen, response to *The Inauguration of the Law of Christ with the Gospel of Christ: A Dispensational View.* by Wayne Strickland in Gundry, Stanley N. ed. *Five Views of Law and the Gospel*, (Grand Rapids: Zondervan, 1996), 299.

to a neighbor; therefore love is the fulfillment of *the* law." The phrase in verse 10, "You shall love your neighbor as yourself" comes from Leviticus 19:18. There is a variation to love strangers in Leviticus 19:34. This passage in Leviticus lists a series of descriptions that explain how an individual ought to act with those with whom he lives. This is a clear Old Testament injunction from the law that everyone agrees is a fundamental duty of Christians. Thus loving others is "the fulfilling of the law."

In Ephesians 6:1-2 and Colossians 3:20 Paul writes a reminder to obey parents in accordance with the fifth commandment.

Look at Paul's explanation of Deuteronomy 25:4 in 1 Corinthians 9:9-10, "For it is written in the Law of Moses, 'You shall not muzzle the ox while he is threshing.' God is not concerned about oxen, is He? Or is He speaking altogether for our sake? Yes, for our sake it was written, because the plowman ought to plow in hope, and the thresher *to thresh* in hope of sharing *the crops.*" God includes this verse in Scripture for our benefit. Paul cites this Old Testament passage from the law as an example to instruct people in their responsibilities toward pastors. God made provision for the ox so he can continue to work. The same is true for Christians. The principle is if an animal is worth having to do work, then it is worth good care. This is even more important where men are concerned for they are more important than animals. "Specific directions contained in the Old Testament, even with regard to beasts and inanimate things, are often illustrations of principles, and are designed to instruct men in all ages as to the character and will of God, and the nature, variety, and extent of human duties."[17]

The law condemns evil speaking: "You shall not go about as a slanderer among your people, and you are not to act against the life of your neighbor; I am the Lord" (Lev. 19:16). The New Testament also warns against such behavior: "Do not speak against one another, brethren.

---

17 Comments on 1 Corinthians 9:10. Family Bible Notes from the Nazarene Users Group. (Tempe, AZ: The Crosswire Software and Bible Society).

He who speaks against a brother or judges his brother, speaks against the law and judges the law; but if you judge the law, you are not a doer of the law but a judge *of it*" (Jam. 4:11). The idea of both passages is that men ought to love one another. The man who continues in that sin disregards the law. By his words and actions, he judges and condemns the law. In effect, he is saying I will make my own law. A biting tongue that defames a brother in Christ condemns the law of God as well as Christ's commandments. The man who considers the law as not worth keeping is living in sin.

The Law says do not commit adultery. Jesus adds to that in Matthew 5:28. "I say to you that everyone who looks at a woman with lust for her has already committed adultery with her in his heart." Christ fulfilled the Law by enhancing its spiritually. Jesus prohibits lust because He deals with motives and attitudes as well as actions.

In 1 Corinthians 14:34–35, Paul instructs women to keep silent in the church, instructing "them ask their own husbands at home." This is a New Testament fulfillment of Genesis 3:16 where God tells Eve, "Yet your desire will be for your husband, and he will rule over you."

The New Testament says we are no longer under the Law for justification. Nevertheless, it gives us all kinds of commands, many of which have roots in the Old Testament. That alone is reason enough for believers to have a love for the law. The Holy Spirit gives God's people a love of the law. Indeed, a love for the law leading to a natural desire to keep its commandments is an indicator of the regeneration of a lost soul. "Those who love Your law have great peace, and nothing causes them to stumble" (Ps. 119:165).

CHAPTER 5

THE PURPOSE OF THE LAW

INTERESTINGLY ENOUGH, THERE IS NO reason given for the Law at Sinai. God calls Moses up the mountain, gives him the law, and tells him to teach it to the people and institute it into the life of the nation. Nevertheless, there is much to learn about God's intentions for the human race from the Old Testament.

One purpose of the law was to demonstrate the graciousness of God. "For you are a holy people to the LORD your God; the LORD your God has chosen you to be a people for His own possession out of all the peoples who are on the face of the earth" (Deut. 7:6).

The law is God's revelation of His character to His chosen people. He revealed His character in Leviticus 11:45, saying, "For I am the Lord who brought you up from the land of Egypt to be your God; thus you shall be holy, for I am holy." Also, Leviticus 19:2 says, "Speak to all the congregation of the sons of Israel and say to them, you shall be holy, for I the Lord your God am holy." Douglas J. Moo writes, "God's character is the implied basis for the entire law."[1] Kaiser agrees, "The law was designed to reveal the character of God to Israel."[2] As a revelation of God's character, the law demands conformity to His character. There are dire punishments, usually death, for breaking the law. The

---

1 Douglas J. Moo, *The Law of Christ as the Fulfillment of the Law of Moses: A Modified Lutheran View*, in Gundry, Stanley N. ed. *Five Views of Law and the Gospel*, (Grand Rapids: Zondervan, 1996), 335.
2 Walter C. Kaiser, Response to Douglas J. Moo in *The Law of Christ as the Fulfillment of the Law of Moses: A Modified Lutheran View*, in Gundry, Stanley N. ed. *Five Views of Law and the Gospel*, (Grand Rapids: Zondervan, 1996), 397.

law stresses the need to separate from unclean things because they are not holy.

PURPOSE OF THE LAW IN THE OLD TESTAMENT

God covenanted with Israel that the law would be a source of blessing if they were obedient. "Therefore, you shall keep the commandment and the statutes and the judgments which I am commanding you today, to do them. Then it shall come about, because you listen to these judgments and keep and do them, that the Lord your God will keep with you His covenant and His lovingkindness which He swore to your forefathers" (Deut. 7:11–12).

"The law gave specific instructions to them [Israel] concerning appropriate behavior within the covenant relationship."[3] The law gave them a requirement for holiness as well as a prescription for forgiveness through the sacrifices. The Psalms reveal that obedience to the law makes it possible for God's chosen people to live in fellowship with their Creator. "In the covenant into which God entered with Israel, He promised to bestow upon them a variety of blessings so long as they continued obedience to Him as their heavenly King . . . The people accordingly were truly happy as a nation, and found every promise which the faithful God made to them amply fulfilled, so long as they adhered to that obedience which was required of them."[4]

The law as a covenant had blessings attached, but receiving the blessings was conditional. God would bless Israel only if they obeyed His commandments. "Now it shall be, if you diligently obey the Lord your God, being careful to do all His commandments which I command you today, the Lord your God will set you high above all the nations of the earth" (Deut. 28:1).

3 Wayne G. Strickland, *The Inauguration of the Law of Christ with the Gospel of Christ: A Dispensational View.* in Gundry, Stanley N. ed. *Five Views of Law and the Gospel,* (Grand Rapids: Zondervan, 1996), 237.

4 Robert Jamieson, A.R. Fausset, David Brown, *Commentary: Practical and Explanatory on the Whole Bible,* new and rev. ed. (Grand Rapids, Michigan: Zondervan, 1961), 147.

God made their future choices and consequences clear with the instructions to have six tribes to recite blessings on Mt. Gerizim. "All these blessings will come upon you and overtake you if you obey the LORD your God" (Deut. 28:2). The remaining tribes recited curses, which were really consequences, on Mt. Ebal. "But it shall come about, if you do not obey the Lord your God, to observe to do all His commandments and His statutes with which I charge you today, that all these curses will come upon you and overtake you" (Deut. 28:15). Unfortunately, Israel frequently failed to obey. Then God brought judgment, famine, pestilence, war, even conquering armies and dispersion from the land, "because they did not obey the voice of the Lord their God, but transgressed His covenant, *even* all that Moses the servant of the Lord commanded; they would neither listen nor do *it*" (2 Kings 18:12).

When Moses reviews Israelite history in Deuteronomy, the events since leaving Egypt, and God's promise to them as a chosen people, He describes the utility of the law for all people. In Deuteronomy 4:1–8, Moses explains that statutes and judgments are essential. He tells them to hearken to what God has to say. The Hebrew word translated *hearken* means to listen intelligently with the intent to obey. God's people have to listen with a heart that is predisposed to obey God. The idea behind the phrase *now therefore hearken* in Deuteronomy 28:1 (KJV) is that men must hear the Word of God. The law is the voice of God, thus the utterance of righteousness.

Moses is warning them to listen, pay attention, and obey God. He understands the urgency of teaching mankind because adherence to rules of order does not come naturally. To obey God's statutes and judgments leads to a long physical life, but much more. God is interested in how men get along with each other, and the law shows them what is right and wrong. "Some things correspond to God's nature; these things are right—absolutely right. Other things conflict with God's nature. These things are wrong—absolutely wrong. The prohibition against murder and adultery demonstrate God's goodness and desire for mankind to live in peace and harmony."[5] Obedience to "everything that proceeds out of the mouth of the Lord" (Deut. 8:3) leads to a higher life, a spiritual life, which pleases God. When men live in a manner that pleases God, they experience the fulfillment of the promises of God.

Moses taught them that God's intention for the law is to give them civil and religious guidelines to follow when they enter the Promised Land. Josephus explained, "He gave them the laws and the constitution of government written in a book." He described the Mosaic Law, "This was the form of political government which was left us by Moses."[6] "So You made known to them Your holy Sabbath, and laid down for them commandments, statutes and law, through Your servant Moses" (Neh. 9:13). If they perform the law, they will live and possess the land that God has given them. The implication is if they do not follow the law, they will die and lose the land. That did in fact happen; the Assyrians conquered the Northern Kingdom followed by Babylon's destruction of Judah.

Moses was speaking to Israel, but the message applies to any great nation. The emphasis here is a foundation on the Word of God, the Holy Bible. Man's whole obligation is to heed the Word of God. Israelites who obeyed received the promise of life and a rich inheritance. The prosperity that results from true piety leading to obedience to the law symbolizes the kingdom that God intended and that will come in the future.

There is one certainty for all men. The law given by Moses is a commandment from Jehovah. It is the will of God that men read and study the Word of God. Its authority is absolute and requires obedience. The statutes and commandments of God are complete. Men need nothing else (Prov. 30:6, Rev. 22:19). Men must not amend or abridge God's laws. The design of the law of God is to have full authority in

---

5 Harold Vaughn, An Unscriptural Division. *The Baptist Examiner.* June 11, 1998, 1, 8, 9.
6 Josephus Antiquities 4.8.3, 4.8.44.

all phases of human life, over the intellect, emotions, morality, every aspect of daily living, indeed over the whole man.

THE LAW WAS A SUPERIOR FORM OF GOVERNMENT

Moses explained that the faithful observance of the law God gave them would raise their national character for intelligence and wisdom.[7] The divine and infinitely wise statutes gave Israel superiority over the surrounding pagan nations.[8] The Law was a depository "of true wisdom and knowledge"[9] and made Israel a light to the Gentiles. Moses instructed Israel: "So keep and do *them*, for that is your wisdom and your understanding in the sight of the peoples who will hear all these statutes and say, 'Surely this great nation is a wise and understanding people'" (Deut. 4:6).

The heathen world generally ridiculed Israel for what they saw as an excessive exclusiveness. Yet, many of their most eminent philosophers and thinkers expressed admiration for the fundamental unity of the nation. The true knowledge and wisdom in the law of God attracted heathen nations. The Queen of Sheba went to Solomon to learn about his wisdom, which was rooted in the law. The Mosaic Law draws pagans who are seeking truth, even though they will reject the God who gave it. Foreign legislators demonstrated their admiration for the Mosaic Law by copying from it to structure their own civil codes, which led to some pagan nations with a high degree of morality.

A nation populated with people who obey God's commandments has the potential for greatness. "Religion and morality are the strength of every civilization."[10] The law provided a code of living that brings

---

7 Meredith G. Kline, *Deuteronomy* in *The Wycliffe Bible Commentary*, ed. Charles F. Pfeiffer and Everett F. Harrison. (Nashville: The Southwestern Co., 1962), 161.
8 Until God gave the law, every nation's laws were wicked, obscene, foolish, and often unjust as they came from the jaded hearts of men.
9 W. L. Alexander, Deuteronomy in *The Pulpit Commentary*, ed. H.D.M. Spence & Joseph Exell. (New York: Funk & Wagnalls, 1913), 58.
10 D. Russell Scott, Deuteronomy in *The Abingdon Bible Commentary*. Frederick C. Eiselen, Edwin Lewis, and David G. Downey, ed. (New York: Abingdon-Cokesbury Press, 1929), 324.

the enjoyment of the blessings of God. The living God of Israel who hears and answers prayer offers a distinctively better approach to building a great nation.

No other nation can match the excellence of the religion grounded in the Mosaic Law because no other religion or legal system contained "statutes and judgments as righteous as this whole law" (Deut. 4:8). The true greatness of a nation is not in military power, the size of its empire, but in the quality and righteousness of its legal system. A nation that follows the moral precepts of the Mosaic Law is a tremendous example to other nations because it practices true wisdom and understanding.

The Mosaic Law placed Israel in a superior situation over all other nations because of their unique relationship with God. "He declares His words to Jacob, His statutes and His ordinances to Israel. He has not dealt thus with any nation; And as for His ordinances, they have not known them. Praise the Lord" (Ps. 147:19-20)! Paul confirmed this relationship: "First of all, they were entrusted with the oracles of God" (Rom. 3:2). The superiority of the Mosaic Law makes a common standard that all people should follow—a divine standard that will work with all nations.

A nation that would have "a wise and understanding people" (Deut. 4:6) must keep and obey the law. Obedience to God's commands gives a good testimony to the heathen. False gods of pagan nations provided no instruction or guidance as complete and perfect as the law of God.

THE LAW IS PRACTICAL

There are many Old Testament passages that illustrate the practical efficacy of the law. The Psalms are replete with references to delighting in the law, obeying the law, and the law as a guide to the believer's life. Much of Psalm 119 reveals the usefulness of the law for living in a manner pleasing to God. One such passage is Psalm 119:9-11, "How can a young man keep his way pure? By keeping *it* according to Your word. With all my heart I have sought You; do not let me wander from

Your commandments. Your word I have treasured in my heart, that I may not sin against You." Those who chose the law as a guide will tend to avoid sinful living. Those who live righteously can say their "delight is in the law of the Lord, and in His law he meditates day and night" (Ps. 1:2).

PURPOSE OF THE LAW IN THE NEW TESTAMENT

God gave the law in the Old Testament with little explanation why. Christians see the larger picture of the plan of God for He used the New Testament writers to explain in detail His purposes for giving the law.

The Law Has a Purpose for Lost Sinners

Ignorance of the Law leads lost sinners into carelessness about their soul. The good news of the gospel is mere foolishness to a lost man. He has no hope until shown the consequences of sin. Only then will the lost reach a state of despair and call upon the Lord Jesus Christ for salvation.

Anything that reduces the impact of the Law reduces the light by which men recognize their guilt. In turn, there is less likelihood of conviction and conversion. Sinners who gain an understanding of the consequences of breaking the law of God realize they cannot escape God's wrath in judgment. In desperation, the lost sinner will see the necessity of repenting and calling upon the Lord Jesus Christ, "who rescues us from the wrath to come" (1 Thess. 1:10). "Everyone must pass through the door of death."[11] "And inasmuch as it is appointed for men to die once and after this *comes* judgment" (Heb. 9:27).

"By the works of the Law no flesh will be justified in His sight; for through the Law *comes* the knowledge of sin" (Rom. 3:20). The law is what determines sin. It shows how men have deviated from God's righteous standard and sentences them to death because they have

---

11 Ray Comfort, "The Preaching of the Law Is Hell's Best Kept Secret." Herald of His Coming, Vol. 48, No. 12, December 1989, 1, 3.

broken it. The law is properly the means for men to discover the full knowledge of sin. For the depraved heart of man will never identify as sin what it enjoys.

"The Law came in so that the transgression would increase" (Rom. 5:20). The law draws attention to every single sin committed under the law, revealing to sinful men their many offenses against God. In showing men their sin, it serves as a guide to the conscience and life. In its spirit and power, it serves men so they can recognize the sin in their lives. The law ensures the true nature, evil, and wickedness of sin become evident "for through the Law *comes* the knowledge of sin" (Rom. 3:20). The law does not show how pathetic men are but reveals their scriptural position of guilt before a holy God. The law of God leaves the sinner with no means of payment before the Judge of the universe; it leaves them in a helpless state before God.

"What shall we say then? Is the Law sin? May it never be! On the contrary, I would not have come to know sin except through the Law; for I would not have known about coveting if the Law had not said, 'You shall not covet'" (Rom. 7:7). The law itself is not sin. It is the means of revealing sin. "For, if it be not brought forth from it lurking places, it miserably destroys in secret before its fatal sting is discerned."[12] The law is the standard used by God to measure the actions of men. Sadly, all men fall far short of God's standard and must suffer eternal punishment, which is death—separation from God. Paul also wrote, "For the Law brings about wrath, but where there is no law, there also is no violation" (Rom. 4:15). Paul is writing of how God established the law to show men just how wicked they are and how virulent is the propensity to sin in the human heart.

"Knowing this, that the law is not made for a righteous man, but for the lawless and disobedient, for the ungodly and for sinners, for unholy and profane, for murderers of fathers and murderers of mothers, for manslayers, For whoremongers, for them that defile themselves with

---

12 John Calvin, *Institutes.* 2.7.6.

mankind, for menstealers, for liars, for perjured persons, and if there be any other thing that is contrary to sound doctrine" (1 Tim. 1:10). He went on to add in verse 11 that the law is "according to the glorious gospel of the blessed God, which was committed to my trust." The law shows us what is opposed to righteous living and sound doctrine and what is in agreement with the gospel. "Viewing the matter from a social standpoint, this is a highly beneficent purpose."[13]

Paul praises the Law, "Wherefore the law is holy, and the commandment holy, and just, and good" (Rom. 7:12). Laws are as the lawmakers are. The character of God, the great Lawgiver, is holy, just, and good; therefore His law must reflect His character. The commandments, indeed, every part of the law is "holy, and just, and good." The law commands holiness for it matches the holy will of God who is the origin of holiness. The law is good in the design of it. The law is for the good of mankind to produce peace and order in the world. The law makes those who observe it good. The law can reform mankind. The psalmist writes, "The law of the Lord is perfect, restoring the soul" (Ps. 19:7). The law is truth, without blemish, complete, full, and perfect, without spot, and undefiled.

The law "springs from, and partakes of, the holy nature of God; it is every way just and right in itself; it is designed wholly for the good of man."[14] This is true because the Law has the purpose of leading men to Christ (Gal. 3:24). The Law as well as "the entire written Word of God is able to make us wise with reference to that salvation which we have by faith in Christ."[15]

In Galatians 3:19 Paul explains further, writing, "Why the Law then? It was added because of transgressions, having been ordained through angels by the agency of a mediator, until the seed would come

---

13 Alva J. McClain, *Law and Grace*. 1954. Reprint, (Chicago: Moody Press, 1967), 25.

14 Comments on Romans 7:12. John Wesley, *John Wesley's Notes on the Bible*. Based on the electronic edition by Sulu Kelley and Bill Brown, (Tempe, AZ: The Crosswire Software and Bible Society).

15 McClain, 55.

to whom the promise had been made." The phrase, *it was added because of transgressions* illustrates how the law was necessary due to the sinful, Adamic nature of man. *It was added* indicates the law was not the first method God had to deal with sinners. The covenants and promises of God were first. Sin so prevailed because the natural desire of men, wallowing in a love of self, wants to sin. Some method of revealing sin was necessary. God gave the law to establish a reference point for the behavior of mankind.

The Law Has a Purpose for Christians

"For whatever was written in earlier times was written for our instruction, so that through perseverance and the encouragement of the Scriptures we might have hope" (Rom. 15:4). The words translated *written in earlier times* refers to the Old Testament for that is the only Scripture available when the Apostle wrote. Through the consolation, which God gives us with these Scriptures, we may have patience and a joyful hope. And, from what He says, we realize that God did not intend for the Old Testament to be only for the generations of Israel before the incarnation, but for the instruction of all the succeeding generations of mankind.

"Now these things happened to them as an example, and they were written for our instruction, upon whom the ends of the ages have come" (1 Cor. 10:11). Paul has just finished writing of the events of the Exodus. Now he says those events are in the Old Testament to be an example, a lesson for believers. The phrase *they are written* means the Exodus is in the Scriptures to serve as practical guidance and instruction for all believers. The Scriptures prove this over and over. The prophets and the writers of the New Testament constantly refer to events in Israel's history as object lessons.

"Now these were more noble-minded than those in Thessalonica, for they received the word with great eagerness, examining the Scriptures daily *to see* whether these things were so. Therefore many of them believed, along with a number of prominent Greek women and men" (Acts 17:11–12). They searched to determine whether the Christian interpretation, which the Apostle put upon the Old Testament Scriptures, was the true one. They searched the Old Testament to see whether the promises and types corresponded with the alleged fulfillment in the person, works, and sufferings of Jesus Christ. After examining the Scriptures, they believed. They believed because their study of the "Law of Moses, and in the prophets, and in the psalms" convinced them that Jesus of Nazareth whom Paul preached was indeed the great Prophet promised in the Old Testament. Their belief comes from their time spent searching the Scriptures. This confirms that faith comes from the Word of God, which is in both Testaments.

The Lord Jesus told the religious leaders to study the Word. At the time of His ministry, all that was available to them was the Old Testament. "You search the Scriptures because you think that in them you have eternal life; it is these that testify about Me" (John 5:39). Jesus gave a clear and unambiguous command to all men to read and study the Old Testament. Sadly, these religious leaders spent much time in study of the Scriptures but did not learn the message of the Word of God. They missed the part where the Scriptures showed that Jesus was the Messiah, and that they must believe in Him or perish.

Ignorance of the Word is perilous. "But Jesus answered and said to them, 'You are mistaken, not understanding the Scriptures nor the power of God'" (Matthew 22:29). The doctrine of the immortality of the soul and of the resurrection of the body is in the Old Testament, as is the obligation of men to love God with all their heart and their neighbors as themselves. Christ revealed these truths with greater clearness in the New, but the requirements of both Testaments are substantially the same.

If the law were invalid, every Old Testament instruction would be invalid in the Church Age. If that were true, it would be evident from Scripture when early church believers stopped obeying the Old Testament and the Law and began using only the New Testament. That never happened. "We are not under the Law; but because that law is inspired Scripture, it is full of valuable doctrine and useful lessons for us."[16]

A PERFECT STANDARD

God has consistently set a high standard of behavior for His people. "And when Abram was ninety years old and nine, the Lord appeared to Abram, and said unto him, I am the Almighty God; walk before me, and be thou perfect" (Gen. 17:1, KJV). The word *perfect* in this verse means to be blameless. God is saying, "Abraham, walk with me and while you are doing so, your life ought to be without blame. In other words, live a perfect life."

Later on God inspired Moses to write these words: "Thou shalt be perfect with the Lord thou God" (Deut. 18:13, KJV). Again *perfect* has the connotation of blameless. God intends for believers to be sincerely and wholly His, seeking Him and cleaving to Him and to His Word alone. Moses was giving instructions to live a blameless, perfect life.

In the Sermon on the Mount, Jesus said, "Be ye therefore perfect, even as your Father which is in heaven is perfect" (Matt. 5:48, KJV). God himself is the only pattern of perfection, which Jesus tells us to pattern ourselves after. The words are very emphatic. "You are to be perfect." The meaning is remarkably similar to those two Old Testament passages. It means complete, conveying the idea of blameless living without any reference to extenuating circumstances—just live perfect. The second perfect in the verse is a reference to God, the faultless Creator. But the first *perfect* in the verse is the same word and is meant as a desired condition for men to emulate.

Apostle Paul emphasizes the godly standard. "Finally, brethren, farewell. Be perfect, be of good comfort, be of one mind, live in peace; and the God of love and peace shall be with you" (2 Cor. 13:11, KJV).

16 McClain, 56.

The word translated *perfect* means believers are to aim for the highest possible level of holiness. God's people must find what is lacking in their Christian character in order to be perfect in the belief and practice of the truth. Living a perfect life before God is what He expects men to do. Sadly, men are stained with sin and incapable of doing so. Nothing has changed from the time of Noah, when "the Lord saw that the wickedness of man was great on the earth, and that every intent of the thoughts of his heart was only evil continually" (Gen. 6:5).

The standard of perfection that God expects men to live up to is set very high. The Old Testament law, which reflects the character of God, is that standard. The law is a perfect instrument designed to lead Israel to ethical perfection.[17] The law was necessary so that men can see the true nature of sin and might be the better prepared to receive the gospel. Sadly, for the unbelieving nation of Israel, the law became a burden that showed their guilt before a holy God and condemned them. "For [the real function of] the Law is to make men recognize *and* be conscious of sin [not mere perception, but an acquaintance with sin which works toward repentance, faith, and holy character]" (Rom. 3:20, Amplified).

The law is a command and has a penalty. The command inwardly stimulates in sinful men an act of rebellion against God. The penalty serves to restrain the outward act of rebellion.

Adam Clarke wrote, "Now, it is wisely ordered of God, that wherever the gospel goes there the law goes also; entering everywhere, that sin may be seen to abound, and that men may be led to despair of salvation in any other way or on any terms but those proposed in the gospel of Christ."[18] If this were not true, no preacher could teach Abraham's willingness to sacrifice Isaac, expound upon the Ten Commandments,

---

17 Willem A. VanGemeren, *The Law is the Perfection of Righteousness in Jesus Christ: A Reformed Perspective.* in Gundry, Stanley N. ed. *Five Views of Law and the Gospel,* (Grand Rapids: Zondervan, 1996), 32.

18 Comments on Romans 5:20. Adam Clarke, *Commentary on the Whole Bible.* (Tempe, AZ: The Crosswire Software and Bible Society, 1810/1825).

or preach the life of David whom God declared "a man after mine heart , who will do all My will" (Acts 13:22). Thus, the knowledge of sin contained in the law is necessary to prompt the sinner to become truly repentant. When men clearly see the curse of the law condemning their soul, they are glad to flee for refuge to the hope found in the gospel. Now "grace abounded all the more," and the sins revealed in the law that condemn souls to death are freely and fully forgiven. The Old Testament standard in the law based on the perfect character of God is still valid as a reference to show lost men their sin.

WHY THE LAW

"Why the Law then? It was added because of transgressions, having been ordained through angels by the agency of a mediator, until the seed would come to whom the promise had been made" (Gal. 3:19). The law was necessary because of the transgressions of the Jews who were so prone to forsake God, worship idols, and commit all sorts of abominations. God gave them the law to be a guide for living, to restrain them from sin. The types, shadows, and figures in the law served to preserve among them the knowledge of Jehovah and the right way to worship Him. The law would show them the folly of sin and their need of a Savior. The law showed Christ, the Messiah, and the salvation He will bring. The law would point them to Christ as "the Lamb of God who takes away the sin of the world" (John 1:29). "For God did not send the Son into the world to judge the world, but that the world might be saved through Him" (John 3:17). "The Law shows the way of condemnation so we will reach out for salvation."[19]

Frequently cited as a purpose of the law is Galatians 3:24, which states, "Wherefore the law was our schoolmaster *to bring us* unto Christ, that we might be justified by faith." The most common understanding is the phraseology of the KJV. This is unfortunate because the italicized words *"to bring us"* added by the translators is misleading.

---

19 Paul Hornung in a sermon preached at Grace Baptist Church, Landrum, SC, on 22 June 2011.

Most modern translations have perpetuated the error by changing it to "lead us to Christ." John Darby's translation is much clearer: "So that the law has been our tutor up to Christ, that we might be justified on the principle of faith."[20]

English Bibles translate the Greek word *pedagogue* as schoolmaster or tutor. A pedagogue is not a schoolmaster but instead a reliable and trustworthy servant hired to care for male children from childhood to puberty. The pedagogue was supposed to keep him from physical harm and immorality. The pedagogue took the child to and from school, helped with his studies, and accompanied him during recreation. A pedagogue did not make the youngster a man. Instead, he was with the child until manhood. Paul's example is that the law was the Jew's pedagogue until Christ came with the gospel. The law is a guide for living until Christ. The law did not bring men to salvation. By its rites, ceremonies, sacrifices, types, and prophecies, it was a guide for living until the gospel.

Galatians 3:25 explains further: "But now that faith has come, we are no longer under a tutor." The faith that came was Christ manifested in the flesh and the gospel He preached. Men no longer need a pedagogue (law) to guide them until the Christ brings the gospel. God enacted the law for the good of the world to show "man the way of obedience and peace, and conduct him to the author of his nature and of the law."[21]

Paul also explains to the Galatians what the Law cannot do. "Is the Law then contrary to the promises of God? May it never be! For if a law had been given which was able to impart life, then righteousness would indeed have been based on law" (Gal. 3:21). It cannot give eternal life. Men cannot depend upon the Law to save them. Instead, the Law convinces men of their need for a Savior. Neither is the Law against the promises of God. A few verses earlier, Paul specifically mentions

---

20 Galatians 3:24 from the *Darby Bible* (1889). A literal translation of the Old Testament (1890) and the New Testament (1884) by John Nelson Darby (1800-82).

21 Comments on Galatians 3:25. Matthew Henry, *Complete Commentary on the Whole Bible*. Public Domain. This text was prepared from the Christian Classics Ethereal Library located at www.ccel.org. (Tempe, AZ: The Crosswire Software and Bible Society).

the promise to Abraham (Gal. 3:16–18) is still valid. The promise is of a Savior to redeem men from their sin, which predates the law by 400 years. Several millennia before that is the first promise of a coming Savior in Genesis 3:15. That promise too, well before the Law, came to fruition in Christ. The Law could only reveal sin and the need for a Savior foretold well before the events at Sinai. The Law cannot give life. If it were possible for the Law to give life, then God would have spared His Son the agony of the cross. Righteousness, or justification and the blessings of God, would have come from the Law. Thus, the Law reveals the sin that men must confess before they can obtain and enjoy the promise of God fulfilled in the Lord Jesus Christ.

Kenneth Wuest summarized Paul's words in Galatians 3:[22]

- God gave the Law to show that sin is more than just submission to evil urges; it's a violation of His Laws.

- God gave the Law so that sinful man could see that his ways were missing the mark of God's standards and recognize the need for a sacrificial substitute to take his punishment. The idea being the sinner would look to the promised Savior found in the prophets who in the future would take his rightful punishment by dying for his sins.

- God gave the Law because the sinner behaves as a selfish child, desiring his own way and flaunting the authority of the Creator. The Law was a basic set of instructions that showed the sinner his inability to live without grace.

THE PURPOSE OF THE LAW FOR EVANGELISM

It is through the law that non-Christians become conscious of sin. "Through the Law *comes* the knowledge of sin" (Rom. 3:20). Only a consciousness of sin makes lost men aware of their need for a Savior.

---

22 Kenneth S. Wuest, *Galatians* in Wuest's *Word Studies in the Greek New Testament for the English Reader*, Vol 1. (Grand Rapids, MI: William B. Eerdmans Publishing Company, 1944, reprint 1978), 26.

"If a non-Christian accepts Jesus Christ without a consciousness of sin, his acceptance will be primed by something other than the convicting work of the Holy Spirit."[23]

The Holy Spirit convicts of sin: "And He, when He comes, will convict the world concerning sin and righteousness and judgment; concerning sin, because they do not believe in Me" (John 16:8-9). He uses the Mosaic Law to do that. Genuine conversion follows genuine repentance, which follows genuine conviction of sin. A conscious awareness of sin reveals to men that they cannot meet God's righteous standard for eternal life with Him.

The Law does not save, but shows the need for salvation. The Law does not make men holy. It reveals the holiness of God and reveals how men fall short of His perfection. The Law exposes man's inability to keep the law. The Law reveals man's need for a Savior. That need is the same in any age. Before the Mosaic Law, godly men walked with God, loved Him, were committed to Him, sought His kingdom, and obeyed Him "by practicing righteousness and blamelessness."[24] Neither the introduction of the law or the coming of Christ changed how men are to live for God. Nothing in redemptive history contradicts or changes the manner in which men become justified. The method of justification does not change. The interaction between God and men does not change from pre-law to era of law. Salvation is by faith. The method is the same in both the Old and New Testaments, before Calvary and in the Church Age.

Israel's unique relationship was not just to the Jews. God graciously provided for the "strangers" in their midst. "The same law shall apply to the native as to the stranger who sojourns among you" (Exod. 12:49). The laws concerning offerings applied to the "house of Israel or of the aliens in Israel who presents his offering" (Lev. 18:18). Paul writes of the ultimate fulfillment of the mixing of Jews and strangers. Jews

23 Douglas M. Mindek, The Law and Evangelism. *Alliance Life*, June 6, 1990, 21.
24 VanGemeren, 19.

and Gentiles who, when saved, are one in Jesus Christ. Their salvation came not by circumcision or baptism but by the blood of Christ. There is no separate plan for Jews and the church. Christ completely fulfills all the demands of the law, thus uniting all people in access to God. Christ reconciled them by dying. He took the hatred between people and nailed it to the cross. There ought not to be any fighting between different groups of believing Christians since they are one in Christ. Christ is our peace because of the work He did at Calvary.

Thus, there is no conflict between Old Testament law and New Testament gospel. The Gospel fulfills the Law. The Gospel contains new covenant commandments, which are required of all believers. The Gospel introduces grace, obedience to Christ, and the leading of the Holy Spirit. When walking in the Spirit, we will never be in conflict with the law.

THE END AND PURPOSE OF THE LAW

Edward Fisher wrote in 1649: "And to this end and purpose, let them consider and mark well the end why the law was given, which was not to bring us to salvation, not to make us good, and so to procure God's love and favor toward us: but rather to declare and convict our wickedness, and make us feel the danger thereof: to this end and purpose, that we seeing our condemnation, and being in ourselves confounded, may be driven thereby to have our refuge in the Son of God, in who alone is to be found our remedy."[25]

---

25 Edward Fisher, "The Marrow of Modern Divinity," ed. Thomas Boston, 1718 in Myron Houghton. *Law and Grace.* (Schaumburg, IL: Regular Baptist Books, 2011), 202.

CHAPTER 6

DIFFERENCES BETWEEN LAW AND GOSPEL

THIS BOOK WOULD BE INCOMPLETE without some discussion about the changes wrought in the New Testament era because of Christ's efficacious work. Our Savior said, "Do not think that I came to abolish the Law or the Prophets; I did not come to abolish but to fulfill" (Matt. 5:17). It is necessary to examine some of the ways He fulfilled the law and to determine if the fulfillment in any way abolished any part of the law.

The Law says, "For all have sinned and fall short of the glory of God" (Rom. 3:23). The Gospel replies, "For the Son of Man has come to seek and to save that which was lost" (Luke 19:10).

The law declares, "Do you not know that the unrighteous will not inherit the kingdom of God" (1 Cor. 6:9). The Gospel replies that believers: "not having a righteousness of my own derived from *the* Law, but that which is through faith in Christ, the righteousness which *comes* from God on the basis of faith" (Phil. 3:9).

The Law condemns, "Cursed is he who does not confirm the words of this law by doing them" (Deut. 27:26). The Gospel atones, "Christ redeemed us from the curse of the Law, having become a curse for us" (Gal. 3:13).

"For the Law was given through Moses; grace and truth were realized through Jesus Christ" (John 1:17).

THE MOSAIC LAW IS INCOMPLETE

The Old Testament is not a full and sufficient revelation. It only pointed to the Messiah. It is an incomplete revelation containing only the law of righteousness consisting of formal directions for worship and living, which is not sufficient for true righteous living. "It could not contain all truth, because when it was written the Jews were not capable of receiving all truth."[1] That does not negate its value. The Old Testament is the foundation for a new covenant for humankind when the Messiah, the Prophet of Moses, finishes His salvific work.

Jeremiah foretold the new covenant: "But this is the covenant which I will make with the house of Israel after those days," declares the Lord, "I will put My law within them and on their heart I will write it; and I will be their God, and they shall be My people" (Jer. 31:33). It is new in that, unlike the old covenant that the people continually broke, this new covenant will not be broken. God will put His law within them, and He will write it on their hearts. Because the law is in their hearts, their new nature will result in a desire to keep the laws and statutes of God. In the old covenant, there were two categories of Jew—believers and unbelievers. In the new covenant, every participant will know the Lord. In the new covenant, there is only one group. It contains only those people who have trusted Christ, received forgiveness for their sins, and have the hope of eternity in glory. True worship and righteousness will occur when the Law is no longer external, but in the hearts of men.

In Romans 8:3 Paul writes of "what the Law could not do." The phrase *could not do* is one Greek word that literally means weak or impotent. In other words, the law is powerless to save sinners. The law cannot save men from the guilt of sin, nor from the dominion of sin. The law cannot provide the power to enable men to keep it. Neither can the law provide a way to recover from breaking it. "May God open

---

1 W. F. Adeney, Matthew, vol. 1 in *The Pulpit Commentary*, ed. H.D.M. (Spence & Joseph Exell. New York: Funk & Wagnalls, 1913), 181.

our eyes to understand that our 'help *comes* from the Lord' (Ps. 121:2). Our only hope is in Him."[2]

LIMITATIONS OF THE LAW

Hypothetically, the Law could save. "Now we know that whatever the Law says, it speaks to those who are under the Law, so that every mouth may be closed and all the world may become accountable to God" (Rom. 3:19). The law did not make men criminals, but proved them so. The law was to show Israel that they were sinners. No man can be justified through the law. The law points man to the need for salvation. The inescapable conclusion is that all men are sinners. All the world is guilty before a holy God.

The law could aggravate our sinful nature into action, but it could not secure its own fulfillment. The law could not save, but Christ on the cross "condemned sin in the flesh" (Rom. 8:3). "For through the Law I died to the Law, so that I might live to God" (Gal. 2:19). Paul explains that through the law he is deeply convinced of his utter sinfulness and helplessness. The consequence of the nature of the law means he is dead to any hope or expectation of help or of salvation from the law. Since the law has no salvation, he must take refuge in Jesus Christ. The gospel makes men dead to the law, and the gospel saves men from death, permitting them to live unto God. Paul writes to the Romans, "For the law of the Spirit of life in Christ Jesus has set you free from the law of sin and of death" (Rom. 8:2).

So, hypothetically, the law could save, but only if men could keep and obey it completely. But, using the law for salvation requires perfect obedience to every single part of it, every "jot and tittle" (Matt. 5:18, KJV). In reality, there is one way and one- way only, for men to attain the righteousness and life found in the law—by faith in the Lord Jesus Christ. "And through Him everyone who believes is freed

---

2 Alva J. McClain, *Law and Grace*. 1954. Reprint, (Chicago: Moody Press, 1967), 23.

from all things, from which you could not be freed through the Law of Moses" (Acts 13:39).

A BETTER COVENANT

Returning to the Mosaic Law is a step backward because of the death and resurrection of Jesus. The new covenant is different from the Mosaic Law, which was the old covenant. The law was a dictator, not a friend. The Gospel is a new and better covenant, because in it God has promised other blessings, to other people, on other conditions, than what the old covenant did.

The new covenant is better than the old. God promised the Jews secular blessings, peculiar to their nation, provided they kept the Law of Moses. Under the new covenant, God promises pardon of sin and final salvation to all mankind when men believe on Jesus Christ.

The Jewish priests, who were fallible, dying men, mediated the old covenant by means of bloody sacrifices, which could not take away sin, make the worshippers perfect, nor gain them entrance into heaven. But the sinless Lord Jesus Christ, who is eternal, who is infinite in wisdom and power, by the sacrifice of Himself has established this new covenant, and by the shedding of His blood has opened the kingdom of heaven to all believers.[3]

The Formula of Concord explains the old covenant: "The Law is properly a divine doctrine, which teaches what is right and pleasing to God, and reproves everything that is sin and contrary to God's will."[4]

Concerning the Gospel, the Formula of Concord shows the fulfillment of Christ's work. "The Gospel teaches what a man who has not kept the law and is condemned by it should believe, namely, that Christ has satisfied and paid for all guilt and without man's merit has

---

3 Comments on Hebrews 7:22. Adam Clarke. *Commentary on the Whole Bible.* (Tempe, AZ: The Crosswire Software and Bible Society, 1810/1825).
4 Formula of Concord, *Epitome*, Art V. 2.

obtained, and won for him forgiveness of sins, the righteousness that avails before God, and eternal life."[5]

The problem was not with the old covenant, but with the people. They could not live up to it. "To remedy this, God gives, not a new law, but a new power to the old Law."[6] The old covenant was external, containing commands—"thou shalt, thou shalt not"—that could only command or prohibit action. It could not cleanse the heart. The old covenant was material; the new is spiritual. The old was written on stone, the new is written in their hearts. "For if that first *covenant* had been faultless, there would have been no occasion sought for a second" (Heb. 8:7). Any fault is in man, not the law.

CHANGED PRIESTHOOD

"Now if perfection was through the Levitical priesthood (for on the basis of it the people received the Law), what further need *was there* for another priest to arise according to the order of Melchizedek, and not be designated according to the order of Aaron" (Heb. 7:11)? The Jews would never ask this question. "They were accustomed to regard the system as perfect. The priesthood was an appointment of God, and they were tenacious of the opinion that it was to be permanent, and that it needed no change."[7] They believed the Levitical priesthood was all that was necessary. The problem was that under the Law, God's standard of access to Him was perfection. Worshippers using the law could not become perfect. The law could not take away sin and make men holy. Something better had to take the place of the law and the priesthood. "(For the Law made nothing perfect), and on the other hand there is a bringing in of a better hope, through which we draw

---

5 Formula of Concord, *Epitome,* Art V. 4.
6 Albert Barnes, *Notes on the Old Testament, Explanatory and Practical, Proverbs – Ezekiel.* ed. F.C. Cook, 14th printing. (Grand Rapids, MI: Baker Book House, 1953, reprint 1978), 225.
7 Albert Barnes, *Notes on the New Testament, Explanatory and Practical,* vol. Hebrews. ed. Robert Frew, 16th printing. (Grand Rapids, MI: Baker Book House, 1949, reprint 1978), 160.

near to God" (Heb. 7:19). The imperfection of the law for salvation was why the priest repeated the sacrifices every day.

F. W. Farrar writes, "The writer of Hebrews regards the priesthood rather than the Law as constituting the basis of the whole Mosaic system."[8] Under it the people received the law. Christ, from the tribe of Judah, is a priest after the order of Melchizedek. He was not part of the Aaronic priesthood, which came from the tribe of Levi. Our Savior pointed out when He gave the Great Commission, "All authority has been given to Me in heaven and on earth" (Matt. 28:18). "Nothing of this sort was in Aaron's hands!"[9]

"For when the priesthood is changed, of necessity there takes place a change of law also" (Heb. 7:12). The Greek word translated *changed* means transposed or in place of. The coming of Christ and subsequently Christianity fulfills the priesthood.

"Then He said, 'Behold, I have come to do Your will.' He takes away the first in order to establish the second" (Heb. 10:9). The word *first* means the Old Testament sacrifices of the law. The sacrifices, along with all the types and shadows, are no longer necessary. The word *second* refers to the Lord Jesus Christ who became a sacrifice for us. He fulfilled the sacrificial part of the law by introducing the gospel. This verse is key to the whole book of Hebrews. That is Jesus came in perfect obedience to God to supply an effective, one-time sacrifice to take the place of the Levitical sacrifices of the Old Testament. The idea is taking away that which would not satisfy—animal sacrifices—and fulfilling it with that which would satisfy—Christ's sacrifice on Calvary.

A large portion of the Levitical code was for the regulation of the priesthood and the religious rites they observed and directed. It naturally follows, then, that part of the law relating to the religious

8 F. W. Farrar, *The Epistle of Paul the Apostle to the Hebrews* in *The Cambridge Bible for Schools and Colleges*, ed. J.J.S. Perowne. (Cambridge: University Press, 1893), 121.
9 William R. Newell. *Hebrews: Verse by Verse.* (Chicago: Moody Press, 1947), 229.

duties, instructions, and regulations for the Aaronic priesthood would be part of the change by fulfillment. "It followed that when they were superseded in their office by one of a wholly different order; the law which had regulated them vanished also, or ceased to be binding."[10]

Changing the priesthood naturally carries with it a change in the manner of worship of God. This is necessary as the law and the priesthood are inseparable. As one goes, so does the other. The change is not the abolition of the entire law, just the fulfillment of that portion involving the Aaronic priesthood and its sacrificial system. There is a new worship, living by faith in the Lord Jesus Christ, trusting in His one-time sacrifice.

Men cannot attain perfection through the flesh (Gal. 3:3). The Law only shows men how unrighteous they are. The sacrifices performed by the Aaronic priesthood under the law do not work for salvation (Gal. 5:6). They cannot save, which is why they had to be fulfilled with a change. The order of the Aaronic priesthood didn't last because the willing sacrifice of Christ did away with the sacrifices required by the Law. Men are no longer obligated to offer sacrifices because Christ made one great sacrifice that men avail themselves of to obtain righteousness. The Apostle aptly writes, "I do not frustrate the grace of God: for if righteousness *come* by the law, then Christ is dead in vain" (Gal. 2:21, KJV). This was what Stephen was referring to when he so angered the Jews in that great sermon that led to his martyrdom (Acts 6:13).

Farrar eloquently describes the advantages of the new covenant by comparing the Levitical priesthood with the Lord Jesus Christ:

> "The descendants of Aaron were but priests; Christ, like
> Melchizedek, was both Priest and King. They were for a time;
> He is a Priest forever. They were but links in a long succession,
> inheriting from forefathers, transmitting to dependents;
> He stands alone, without lineage, without successor. They

10 Barnes, vol. Hebrews, 161.

were established by a transitory ordinance, He by an eternal oath. They were sinful. He is sinless. They were weak. He is all-powerful. Their sacrifices were ineffectual. His was perfect. Their sacrifices were offered daily; His once for all. Theirs did but cleanse from ceremonial defilement; His purged the conscience. Their tabernacle was but a copy, and their service a shadow; His tabernacle was the Archetype, and His service the substance. They died and passed away; He sits to intercede for us forever at God's right hand. Their Covenant is doomed to abrogation; His, founded on better promises to endure unto the End. Their high priest could but enter once and that with awful precautions, with the blood of bulls and goats into a material shrine; He, entering with the blood of His one perfect sacrifice into the Heaven of Heavens, has thrown open to all the right of continual and fearless access to God."[11]

The change in the priesthood did not apply to any other part of the law that did not depend upon the appointment of the Levitical priest, specifically that part of the law that directs God's people toward righteous and obedient living.

THE LAW NAILED TO THE CROSS

There was a Jewish custom that upon fulfilling a contract, the one who paid the bill would drive a nail through the document. Paul mentioned that in his letter to the Colossian church: "When you were dead in your transgressions and the uncircumcision of your flesh, He made you alive together with Him, having forgiven us all our transgressions, having canceled out the certificate of debt consisting of decrees against us, which was hostile to us; and He has taken it out of the way, having nailed it to the cross" (Col. 2:13–14).

---

11 Farrar, 147-148.

Christ's death and resurrection wiped away, in fact obliterated, the legal obligation residing in the Law. Christ met the standards of the law for us and satisfied both the precept and penalty of the law. The nails that pierced Christ figuratively pierced the legal document, rendering it null and without force.

The death of Christ not only rendered the Law useless as a means of salvation, but in the rending of the Temple veil, also gave public demonstration that it was so. "God has forever removed the barrier which stood between mankind and Himself."[12] The legal age was terminated. The removal of Jewish obligation to the law is permanent.

Christians are forgiven. Along with the obligation to live by the law, the believer's sins were nailed to the cross with Christ. They are blotted out as soon as the believer has faith in the operation of God. Thus, Jesus has already been victorious over Satan and in the Christian's life. Our guilt is wiped away and nailed to the cross!

OBLIGATION TO THE LAW IS REMOVED

All men have broken the law. But much worse, all men are also under an obligation to suffer the death penalty for breaking the law. "Now we know that whatever the Law says, it speaks to those who are under the Law, so that every mouth may be closed and all the world may become accountable to God" (Rom. 3:20). The word *accountable* means answering for their guilt in breaking the law.

The Law says do such and such and you will live. No man can do it. The first century Jews were looking for a Savior who would free them from bondage to the Romans. They missed the point. The deliverance the law promised was not political, but spiritual. In reality, they were in bondage to sin.

Christ has already done what is necessary for Christians to live in freedom from the penalty of the law. The ceremonies and rituals of

---

12 G. G. Findlay, Colossians in *The Pulpit Commentary*, ed. H.D.M. Spence & Joseph Exell. (New York: Funk & Wagnalls, 1913) 4.

the Law were a decree that works against all mankind. Calvary did not nullify the law; it rescues believers from being held accountable for breaking the law. Christ fulfilled the ordinances of the law and then removed the condemnation of the law, which died with Him (Heb. 10:17–18). He did it to deliver all men, Jew and Gentile alike.

GRACE TEMPERS THE LAW

"You shall love the Lord your God with all your heart and with all your soul and with all your might" (Deut. 6:5). These words place an obligation on mankind. The opening words, *you shall,* make it a command. It is difficult and, for unrepentant men, impossible to love God. Look at how this command is dealt with in the New Testament. First John 4:19 states: "We love, because He first loved us." This is the language of grace. In the Old Testament, we are ordered to love God. In the New Testament, after we experience His love first, we are able to reciprocate and love the Lord God. The passage in Deuteronomy leads men to a Great White Throne Judgment. John's words lead us to the marriage supper.

Leviticus 19:18 says, "You shall love your neighbor as yourself." A difficult command because some people are not lovable. Notice the difference in the New Testament: "Beloved, if God so loved us, we also ought to love one another" (1 John 4:11). Now men have a gracious, God-directed example from the indwelling Holy Spirit.

"In everything, therefore, treat people the same way you want them to treat you, for this is the Law and the Prophets" (Matt. 7:12). By tying this to the Law and Prophets, Jesus implies this is a command. Human nature being what it is, most people will practice this in order to get something good from others. The New Testament takes it to a higher plane. "Do nothing from selfishness or empty conceit, but with humility of mind regard one another as more important than yourselves" (Phil. 2:3). The KJV states, "Let each esteem other better than themselves." What an application of practical grace! Now, this law is an internal motive, driven by the Spirit. The New Testament way is a way of grace.

Four times Paul writes, "We are not under law but under grace" (Rom. 6:15).[13] The Christian's deliverance from the lordship of sin depends upon his deliverance from the law. The law is for fleshly men and their fleshly works, not for righteous men. Using the law, the accuser of the brethren can rightly argue the guilt of men. After the sacrifice on Calvary, the guilt of sinful men is hidden under the blood. The accuser has no case.

The law still serves the purpose convicting and restraining ungodly men. To the Christian, the Law as a legal instrument requiring obedience does not exist. Christ satisfied and fulfilled it. For the Christian, the Law as inspired Scripture is profitable in every part. A true Christian, saved by the grace of God, can delight in all the Word of God. Believers who have seen their sin and learned of their doom can rejoice in assurance of redemption by the Lamb of God.

"The Law made nothing perfect" (Heb. 7:19). "For what the Law could not do, weak as it was through the flesh, God did: sending His own Son in the likeness of sinful flesh and *as an offering* for sin, He condemned sin in the flesh, so that the requirement of the Law might be fulfilled in us, who do not walk according to the flesh but according to the Spirit" (Rom. 8:3–4).

---

13 The others are Romans 6:14, Galatians 5:18, and 1 Corinthians 9:20. The phrase in 1 Corinthians 9:20 is not in the KJV, but is in every other translation.

CHAPTER 7

A NEW COVENANT

CHRIST FULFILLED THE OLD TESTAMENT law in believers, and the prophet Jeremiah who penned these words in chapter 31:31–34 laid out very clearly how it would happen:

> ³¹"Behold, days are coming," declares the Lord, "when I will make a new covenant with the house of Israel and with the house of Judah,

> ³²Not like the covenant which I made with their fathers in the day I took them by the hand to bring them out of the land of Egypt, My covenant which they broke, although I was a husband to them," declares the Lord.

> ³³"But this is the covenant which I will make with the house of Israel after those days," declares the Lord, "I will put My law within them and on their heart I will write it; and I will be their God, and they shall be My people.

> ³⁴They will not teach again, each man his neighbor and each man his brother, saying, 'Know the Lord,' for they will all know Me, from the least of them to the greatest of them," declares the Lord, "for I will forgive their iniquity, and their sin I will remember no more."

These four verses are among the most important in the Old Testament. The phrase "new covenant" is the first introduction of

Christianity. One scholar declares, "The concept of the new covenant to be Jeremiah's most important contribution to biblical thought."[1] Scholars consider this passage as the source of the distinction that gave Christendom the two parts of the Bible: Old Covenant (Testament) and New Covenant (Testament). Paul wrote the apostles are "servants of a new covenant" (2 Cor. 3:6).

This is one of the first places in the Bible to show the difference between the Law and Gospel. The Law shows duty; the Gospel brings the grace of regeneration. Under the new covenant, the heart is changed and the serious believer receives an inner desire for worship and obedience to the Savior.

Six times in this passage, God says, "I will . . . " This indicates He is taking the initiative with the introduction of the new covenant. God truly cares for His people, and this indicates He is taking steps to restore them into fellowship with Him.

The key phrase in this verse is *make a new covenant*. The Hebrew word translated *new* means fresh or unheard of. The word translated *make* as used here means a solemn ratification of a grant or agreement.

"It is new because it was revealed in a new manner, more fully and particularly, plainly and clearly."[2] It was new in a fuller and more spiritual manner because it is spiritual, not material. It is inward, not outward. "The new covenant is a promise, is the assurance indeed, that God has taken the matter of our salvation into His own hands. It is all of grace; He gives everything; nothing is left to our own solitary effort."[3] The need for the replacement of the old covenant shows the real need for what the new covenant provides—"a new power in the hearts of men."[4]

---

1 John F. Graybill, *Jeremiah in The Wycliffe Bible Commentary*, ed. Charles F. Pfeiffer and Everett F. Harrison. (Nashville: The Southwestern Co., 1962), 679.

2 Commentary on Jeremiah 31:31. John Wesley. *John Wesley's Notes on the Bible.* Based on the electronic edition by Sulu Kelley and Bill Brown, (Tempe, AZ: The Crosswire Software and Bible Society).

3 S. Conway, Jeremiah, vol. 11 in *The Pulpit Commentary*, ed. H.D.M. Spence & Joseph Exell. (New York: Funk & Wagnalls, 1913), 37.

4 D. Young, Jeremiah, vol. 11 in *The Pulpit Commentary*, ed. H.D.M. Spence &

SAME PROMISE AS THE OLD COVENANT

It is not a new covenant because it was different in substance and promise from the old. This was the same covenant made with Abraham in Genesis 17:7: "I will establish My covenant between Me and you and your descendants after you throughout their generations for an everlasting covenant, to be God to you and to your descendants after you." It was the same covenant made with the Israelites in Deuteronomy 26:17–18. "You have today declared the Lord to be your God, and that you would walk in His ways and keep His statutes, His commandments and His ordinances, and listen to His voice. The Lord has today declared you to be His people, a treasured possession, as He promised you, and that you should keep all His commandments." The old covenant was on stone. The new covenant will be in their hearts. It will not be a new law for the old law was still good, but it will produce a new heart, which will give men a new motivation to obey the law of God.

The covenant God made with them upon coming out of Egypt was His promise and fixed arrangement for the future of the nation. On God's part, it was the Law he gave through Moses along with His promises to them. Their part was their promise to obey the Law. There was deliverance from Egypt; now a new deliverance must come.

With the old covenant God required obedient actions on the part of His people. The old covenant was a perfect system of morals. "The Law is holy, and the commandment is holy and righteous and good" (Rom. 7:12). Adam and Eve as well as every human since could not obey when faced with a covenant dependent upon human behavior and works. Corrupt human nature, overcome with sin, meant Israel could not obey the law. Salvation by such a method was impossible. But, God is merciful to His people and made a new way to ensure their salvation. The new covenant is one of God giving to His people. The writer of Hebrews explains that Jeremiah is speaking of God

Joseph Exell. (New York: Funk & Wagnalls, 1913), 46.

giving them "a better covenant, which has been enacted on better promises" (Heb. 8:6).

NEW COVENANT IS SPIRITUAL

"It is new because it was revealed in a new manner, more fully and particularly, plainly and clearly."[5] It was new in a fuller manner because it is spiritual, not material. It was inward, not outward. "The new covenant is a promise, is the assurance indeed, that God has taken the matter of our salvation into His own hands. The need for the replacement of the old covenant shows the real need for what the new covenant provides—a new power in the hearts of men."[6]

The problem was not with the old covenant, but the people. They could not live up to the old. "To remedy this, God gives, not a new law, but a new power to the old Law."[7] The old covenant was external, containing commands "thou shalt, thou shalt not," which could only command or prohibit action. It was a dictator, not a friend. It could not cleanse the heart. The old covenant was material; the new would be spiritual. The old was written on stone; the new is written in their hearts.

Jehovah declares this will happen when Elohim says He will be their God. "They shall be My people, and I will be their God" (Jer. 32:38). "The relationship between God and His people is protected from all risk by God Himself making the people what He would have them to be."[8]

NEW COVENANT IS THE GOSPEL

There was a Hebrew custom requiring blood when men agreed to a covenant. Christ alluded to this at the Last Supper when He described

---

5 Commentary on Jeremiah 31:31. Wesley.
6 Young, 46.
7 Albert Barnes, *Notes on the Old Testament, Explanatory and Practical, Proverbs – Ezekiel. ed. F.C. Cook*, 14th printing. (Grand Rapids, MI: Baker Book House, 1953, reprint 1978), 225.
8 T. K. Cheyne, Jeremiah, vol. 11 in *The Pulpit Commentary*, ed. H.D.M. Spence & Joseph Exell. (New York: Funk & Wagnalls, 1913), 14.

the wine as "My blood of the covenant, which is poured out for many for forgiveness of sins" (Matt. 26:28). The writer of Hebrews confirms this: "Now the God of peace, who brought up from the dead the great Shepherd of the sheep through the blood of the eternal covenant, *even* Jesus our Lord" (Heb. 13:20). In this verse, *covenant* means the gospel of Christ.

Jeremiah is writing of a future day when Jehovah God, the glorious and fearful Supreme God, will orchestrate His immutable purposes and promises. He will ratify an agreement with Israel and Judah, indeed, with all mankind who call upon the Lord Jesus Christ in faith. This agreement will be something unheard of in the Old Testament economy. The new covenant is not between God and man, but between God and man's representative, the Lord Jesus Christ. The new covenant will be the gospel of the Lord Jesus Christ. God will ratify the promise with the blood that Christ will shed on Calvary for the eternal salvation of men.

"The foundation of the new covenant is the free forgiveness of sin."[9] Men will realize the complete unmerited love of Christ when they receive His pardon for sins and are forgiven and justified. Properly acknowledged, the love of Christ will place in the heart the desire for obedience.

When they come to know God, He will pardon their unrighteousness and injustice toward others, as well as their wickedness, perversity, and lawlessness. They are forgiven. God will have no recollection of their sin. Forgiven of sins, to be remembered no more, what a great and glorious promise!

A PROMISE TO KNOW GOD

There is another great promise here. They will know God! "It is written in the prophets, 'and they shall all be taught of God.' Everyone who has heard and learned from the Father, comes to Me" (John 6:45).

9 Barnes, 226.

This describes the individual aspect of the new covenant, which is yet another reason the new covenant is a better promise. It is to each man and woman, not to a nation. "It shall be a time of universal light and knowledge; all shall know God in Christ, from the least to the greatest."[10] They will know Him because He put His Word in their heart. When writing of the righteous reign of the Branch, Isaiah pens these words, "For the earth will be full of the knowledge of the Lord as the waters cover the sea" (Isa. 11:9). This is not speaking of evangelism. The new covenant will no longer require the need for a generous, compassionate people like the Thessalonian church to teach brotherly love (1 Thess. 4:9). This is a reference to something new and different where all sins are forgiven and forgotten. Evangelism and missions will be no more.

"The law shows duty, the Gospel brings the grace of regeneration, by which the heart is changed and enabled for duty."[11] Jeremiah is foretelling a time when "God will be truly their God, received and acknowledged as their portion, and the sole object of their devotion; and they shall be his people, filled with holiness, and made partakers of the divine nature, so that they shall perfectly love him and worthily magnify his name."[12] God will preserve His law in the hearts of His people for all eternity. With God's law in their hearts, they will live in holiness to the Lord. They will have full understanding of the Law, the Prophets, and the Writings.

This is not just an Old Testament concept for the Jews. As is often the case, the New Testament explains and expounds on the Old Testament. Paul does this in Romans 8:2-4 where he shows how Christ fulfilled the righteousness of the law and we are to do the same:

> [2]For the law of the Spirit of life in Christ Jesus has set you free from the law of sin and of death.

---

10 Commentary on Jeremiah 31:34. Adam Clarke. *Commentary on the Whole Bible.* (Tempe, AZ: The Crosswire Software and Bible Society, 1810/1825).
11 Comments on Jeremiah 31:33. Wesley.
12 Comments on Jeremiah 31:33. Clarke.

³For what the Law could not do, weak as it was through the flesh, God *did:* sending His own Son in the likeness of sinful flesh and as an *offering* for sin, He condemned sin in the flesh

⁴So that the requirement of the Law might be fulfilled in us, who do not walk according to the flesh but according to the Spirit.

The gospel frees men from the law of sin and death found in the Mosaic Law. The law requires that men become righteous. This cannot happen without deliverance from the condemning power of the law. When Christ saves, the new life with the indwelling Holy Spirit leads Christians to a fulfilled life that is far greater than the sin nature the law exposes.

CHRIST FULFILLED THE LAW IN BELIEVERS

Paul links the Lord Jesus fulfilling the law in Himself and the way in which He fulfills the law in Christians. Christ fulfills the righteousness of the law and we, His people, are to live in such a manner that we do the same. That is possible because we have the Holy Spirit. Yes, sin and death are still present in all men, waging war against the mind and making them prisoners of the law of sin (Rom. 7:23). Joyously, the redeemed have the Holy Spirit, one-third of the Triune Godhead, dwelling within, giving believers a love of the law and the power to live obediently, pleasing God.

"Paul spoke of our 'fulfilling' the intent of the law instead of actually 'doing' the law."[13] Believers become righteous because Christ took their place as a sinner perfectly fulfilling and satisfying the righteous demands of the law. "So that the requirement of the Law might be fulfilled in us, who do not walk according to the flesh but according to the Spirit" (Rom. 8:4).

---

13 Ken Casillas, *The Law and the Christian.* (Greenville, SC: Bob Jones University Press, 2007), 68.

To the Galatians, Paul warned against the doing of the law. "You have been severed from Christ, you who are seeking to be justified by law; you have fallen from grace" (Gal. 5:4). Attempting to be justified under the Law is tantamount to abandoning freedom. Trusting in the Law has no effect. Trusting in Christ and some other thing is of no effect. It must be Christ only, "For if they which are of the law *be* heirs, faith is made void, and the promise made of none effect" (Rom. 4:14). By choosing to follow the law or some other work devised by men, they make it impossible for Christ to work in them. They have erected a barrier to the working of the Holy Spirit in their lives. They become ineffective as Christians. They are still justified, but the ongoing process of sanctification ceases.

A physical action has no spiritual value. What matters is an active, energized faith, expressed and working through love. "Owe nothing to anyone except to love one another; for he who loves his neighbor has fulfilled *the* law. For this, 'You shall not commit adultery, You shall not murder, You shall not steal, You shall not covet,' and if there is any other commandment, it is summed up in this saying, 'You shall love your neighbor as yourself.' Love does no wrong to a neighbor; therefore love is the fulfillment of *the* law" (Rom. 13:8–10).

The Israelites obeyed these commandments as a thing God required them to do. Christians, living by faith with the indwelling Holy Spirit, still obey these commandments, but not as an action. They obey because of a changed heart.

The Mosaic Law is still in effect, still valid, and still part of God's plan of the ages. The difference in the Church Age is that men no longer have to vainly struggle to obey something that is impossible to obey. Now the law is written in the hearts of believers. This took place when the Lord Jesus Christ suffered the punishment believers deserve and declared those who trust Him righteous. Under the new covenant the Holy Spirit enables men to keep the principles of the law, live obediently, and please God.

CHAPTER 8

FULFILLMENT OF THE LAW

DURING HIS EARTHLY MINISTRY, JESUS preached and taught the Old Testament. Yet, many of His opponents accused Him of breaking away from the Old Testament system. Even some of His disciples thought He was teaching a new religion that differed from Judaism. Jesus warned against this idea. It was not His purpose to create a new religion. He counseled that breaking away from the tenets of the Old Testament would be a serious mistake. "Whoever then annuls one of the least of these commandments, and teaches others *to do* the same, shall be called least in the kingdom of heaven; but whoever keeps and teaches them, he shall be called great in the kingdom of heaven" (Matt. 5:19). Everything Jesus did revealed great reverence for the Old Testament Scriptures and Judaism.

The same question that divided the religious leaders of Jesus' day still generates tremendous debate among Christians in this era. Did Jesus intend to do away with the Old Testament religious system? Many believers claim they are under grace, not law, to support a position that the law is no more. The confusion persists even though Jesus frequently declared the Old Testament law was divine.

By its very nature, Judaism was provisional until something better came. "For, on the one hand, there is a setting aside of a former commandment because of its weakness and uselessness (for the Law made nothing perfect), and on the other hand there is a bringing in of a better hope, through which we draw near to God" (Heb. 7:18–19). Despite the many instances of the Spirit aiding the prophets, priests,

123

and patriarchs to provide spiritual assistance and leadership, the Old Testament law itself had no Spirit to minister, required perfect obedience, and did not give any assistance to those who lived under it. "Not only did the Old Testament set forth a typical economy, which must give place to another, but it embodied ethical elements of a provisional kind which must pass away when the incarnate Son had fully revealed the Father."[1] The Mosaic Law had imperfections because it only reveals sin. The sacrifices only covered sin temporarily. The law was incapable of saving from sin or giving peace.

Jesus built upon Judaism. In His own words, Jesus said, "You worship what you do not know; we worship what we know, for salvation is from the Jews" (John 4:22). Even so, the Jewish religion is not adequate to satisfy the needs of the world.

The scribe Jesus described as "not far from the kingdom of God" quoted Deuteronomy 6:5, "and to love Him with all the heart and with all the understanding and with all the strength, and to love one's neighbor as himself." Then the scribe added these words, "is much more than all burnt offerings and sacrifices" (Mark 12:33–34). The principle contained in those added words is an acknowledgment by a lawyer of Judaism that the gospel would replace the sacrificial system.

Human history is a process of revelation of the plan of God. "The Old Testament represents the first steps in a great course of revelation and redemption which reaches its consummation in Christ Himself."[2] Jesus' preaching and teaching in the Gospel was the next step of the process of revelation that God set in motion "before the foundation of the world" (Eph. 1:4).

1 William Caven, The Testimony of Christ to the Old Testament, in *The Fundamentals*, vol. 1 R. A. Torrey, ed. reprint 1996, (Grand Rapids, MI: Baker Books, 1917), 209.
2 George B. Stevens, Gospel and Law in the Teaching of Jesus Christ. *Searching Together*, Spring/Autumn 1992, 9-16.

PROPHETS FORETOLD A COMING CHANGE

This agrees with what the prophets wrote. They heard from God, and some of what they heard caused them to recognize their religion would change. They predicted its alteration into something far better. No other religion has ever foretold its own end the way Judaism did with the foretelling of the coming changes in the new covenant. That fact alone gives credence to the Scriptures.

They sought for a Messiah who would bring a more complete form of the kingdom of God. Jesus described how those who were spiritually discerning in Israel were looking for the emergence of something greater: "For truly I say to you that many prophets and righteous men desired to see what you see, and did not see *it*, and to hear what you hear, and did not hear *it*" (Matt. 13:17). A Messiah was coming, but they were unsure of all it portended.

They unquestioningly prophesied the Word of God even though they did not fully understand the message. "As to this salvation, the prophets who prophesied of the grace that *would come* to you made careful searches and inquiries, seeking to know what person or time the Spirit of Christ within them was indicating as He predicted the sufferings of Christ and the glories to follow" (1 Peter 1:10–11). The prophets of old did not know all the details of the miracle of salvation, but they did know there was a plan for something else. Isaiah must have puzzled greatly over statements about bringing light to the Gentiles.[3] He and the other prophets understood that God would change Judiasm, and they searched for what it would be.

Moses spoke of a Prophet to come they should listen to. "I will raise up a prophet from among their countrymen like you, and I will put My words in his mouth, and he shall speak to them all that I command him" (Deut. 18:18). Here Moses writes that God will raise up a Prophet who is a man. The word translated *Prophet* is singular. It can only mean one person, the Lord Jesus Christ, the Messiah. Christ is a

---

3 Isaiah 42:6, 49:6, 60:3.

true man but also a Prophet of God. The Prophet will speak the words of God. The Old Testament writers anticipated a new and additional revelation when the Messiah came. This prophecy was well known in Judea. "Philip found Nathanael and said to him, 'We have found Him of whom Moses in the Law and *also* the Prophets wrote—Jesus of Nazareth, the son of Joseph'" (John 1:45).

Daniel wrote of the change coming with the Messiah: "I kept looking in the night visions, and behold, with the clouds of heaven One like a Son of Man was coming, and He came up to the Ancient of Days and was presented before Him. And to Him was given dominion, glory and a kingdom, that all the peoples, nations and *men of every* language might serve Him. His dominion is an everlasting dominion which will not pass away; and His kingdom is one which will not be destroyed" (Dan. 7:13–14).

Zechariah knew the coming Messiah would bring change to the Jewish order of things. "And the Lord will be king over all the earth; in that day the Lord will be *the only* one, and His name *the only* one" (Zech. 14:9). Now there are many gods, but in that great future day, all men will unanimously recognize only Jehovah as worthy of worship. False gods and false ways of worship will no longer exist. The kingdom of God shall be a universal and united kingdom. God will possess the hearts of his subjects. Everyone will acknowledge him King. His authority shall be submitted to, and allegiance sworn to Him.

The message of the fulfilled Law, which is the Gospel, now is far fuller and clearer than it was when given to Israel of Old. "As many New Testament authors emphasize, the Christian should read the law as a witness to the fulfillment of God's plan in Christ."[4]

---

4 Douglas J. Moo, *The Law of Christ as the Fulfillment of the Law of Moses: A Modified Lutheran View.* In Gundry, Stanley N. ed. *Five Views of Law and the Gospel*, (Grand Rapids: Zondervan, 1996), 376.

OLD TESTAMENT IS PART OF THE GOSPEL BY FULFILLMENT

It is important to note that Christ fulfilled the whole law, not a part of it. After Christ fulfilled the Mosaic Law, it changed into something better. Christ did not negate or abolish the Law, but fulfilled and completed what it began. The rites and ceremonies He fulfilled with His incarnation, death, and resurrection. The moral aspects He fulfilled with the introduction of the Law of Christ, which is to love God and love your neighbor as yourself. Currently, the judicial statutes are temporarily set aside because Israel is no longer a theocratic nation since Jerusalem fell in 72AD. The Millennium when Christ rules the earth in His perfect righteousness with absolute authority and power (Isa. 11, Micah 4:3) will see the fulfillment of the judicial edicts. Nothing here supports the idea of the law having three parts as used by some theologians. That is inadequate because it divides something that God considered whole.[5] The law does not have separate parts, but different sections of the whole.

That is the biblicist view and the only view naturally found in Scripture. There is no other position that adequately explains the relationship between the Testaments. A system of theology that heavily emphasizes the Mosaic Law as still valid does not know what to do with the ceremonial rites. A system of theology that declares the Mosaic Law invalid has problems with Old Testament principles that Christ and the apostles refer to and teach as important for believers. Christ replaced Moses and offered the Jews a kingdom maintained by spiritual principles, which they rejected. Despite their refusal to accept the Law of Christ, it will one day be written on their hearts.

The old covenant found in the Law "used to be a mere code of morals, external to man, and obeyed as a duty: in Christianity it becomes

---

5 Some theologians divide the law into three separate parts: moral, ceremonial, and judicial sections. This book rejects that idea; see the section titled Divisions of the Law in Chapter 4.

an inner force, shaping man's character from within."[6] God's people can only conclude that the whole Old Testament system, every part of it, is part of the process of fulfillment. Everything in the Old Testament has permanent value and validity. The gospel is the Old Testament fulfilled. As taught so ably by Paul, there is no need to supplement the Christian religion with anything from the Jewish religion. At the same time, there is no need to leave the Old Testament out of preaching because it gives men a consciousness of sin. One who preaches only the hope of the gospel without a message that convicts of sin produces decisions, but no conversion.

It is worth repeating—the Old Testament is part of the gospel by fulfillment. It is vitally important to remember the distinction between destroyed, abolished, abrogated, and fulfilled. Christ fulfilled the Old Testament. He did not destroy, abrogate, abolish, or otherwise do away with it. He fulfilled it. Fulfillment is the only solution to the question of what to do with the Old Testament in the Gospel Age.

Fulfillment is a conserving process. It leaves nothing useful out. When Christ fulfilled the Old Testament, it remained in the message from God as valuable for believers. "The believer is not under the Old Testament system, or, to state the case more fully, he is under only so much of it as has been taken up and incorporated into Christianity, and he is under that because it is part of the Gospel, not because it is a part of the Old Testament religion."[7] Those portions of the Old Testament fulfilled in the Gospel are binding on all believers.

Paul writes in 2 Corinthians 3:9–10, "For if the ministry of condemnation has glory, much more does the ministry of righteousness abound in glory. For indeed what had glory, in this case has no glory because of the glory that surpasses *it*." The "ministry of condemnation" is the law. The "ministry of righteousness" is the gospel message,

6 Albert Barnes, *Notes on the Old Testament, Explanatory and Practical, Proverbs – Ezekiel.* ed. F.C. Cook, 14th printing. (Grand Rapids, MI: Baker Book House, 1953, reprint 1978), 225-226.
7 Stevens, 9-16.

which imparts righteousness by the Holy Spirit. The "ministry of condemnation" lost its glory when fulfilled by the gospel because of the surpassing glory of the gospel. The purpose of the Old Testament was to prepare men for a more perfect system. The true glory of the Old Testament is the great thing to which it pointed. The glory of the Old Testament also teaches the notion that it would decay in order to become even better in its fulfillment.

Tragically, many converted Jews in the apostolic age could not see this. They were unable to throw off the old ways in order to worship the same God. Imagine how much easier it would have been to evangelize the world if they could have understood that Judaism was now fulfilled in Christ: "Jesus has become the guarantee of a better covenant" (Heb. 7:22). Our Savior warned of this problem when He said, "and no one, after drinking old *wine* wishes for new; for he says, The old is good *enough*" (Luke 5:39). Yet, believers so often prefer the old. It took a vision for Peter to understand there was a new covenant. Even then, he was not consistent and Paul had to take him to task. The whole argument concerning circumcision must have tried Paul's soul. He boldly had to declare the Christian is not under law though he never said the law was abolished. Today, just as in Paul's era, there are believers who take the words Paul used to resolve the issue of reliance on the law to justify using works done by man as if the law were still valid.

JESUS IS THE FULFILLMENT OF THE OLD TESTAMENT LAW

For millennia, the hope of the nation of Israel pointed in the direction of a great satisfying completion that would expand the kingdom of God. Jesus fulfilled the hope of Jewish history and ushered in the finale of true revealed religion. Though the religious professionals refused to recognize it, the genesis of the expansion of the kingdom of God they were looking for was in their midst.

The most important passage on this issue is the central theme of this book. "Do not think that I came to abolish the Law or the Prophets; I did not come to abolish but to fulfill" (Matt. 5:17). In the very next verse Jesus says, "For truly I say to you, until heaven and earth pass away, not the smallest letter or stroke shall pass from the Law until all is accomplished" (Matt. 5:18). *Letter* or *stroke* is the familiar jot and tittle of the KJV. Those words alone seem to indicate everything in the Mosaic Law will last in perpetuity. However, verse 18 ends with this phrase, "until all is accomplished" or "all things be fulfilled" (KJV). Jesus is not saying that every part of the Law will last forever, never passing away. He is saying that every part of the Law has to undergo the process of fulfillment. "It shall not pass away till, having served its providential purpose; it is fulfilled in the Gospel."[8]

Understanding how this happens is not simple. It requires thorough study of the New Testament without the blinders imposed by a theological system. The short answer is the law was only the outline of a great plan, the shadow of the glorious gospel to come. Jesus fulfilled the Law by completing or accomplishing what is incomplete in the Law. "The entire Mosaic Law comes to fulfillment in Christ." Everything found in the Law that is interim, temporary, or unnecessary to the perfect Christian religion is no more. Everything that is permanent and essential remains as a permanent part of Christianity.[9]

How Jesus fulfilled the law is twofold. First, He perfectly fulfilled the law by living a righteous life, which is exactly what the law demanded. In Matthew 5:20, Jesus says that righteousness must surpass that of the scribes and Pharisees who held to a scrupulous adherence of the letter of the law but ignored the true spirit of the law. In the following verses (Matt. 5:21–22), Jesus points out obedience to the commandment *Thou shall not kill* is much more than avoiding the actual taking of life. Fully keeping the commandment means to refrain from the anger and hatred in the heart that leads to the act of murder. The

---

8 Stevens, 9-16.
9 Moo, 343.

law covers only overt acts—the physical act of murder. The fulfillment of "thou shall not kill" is true Christianity, which covers the passions of the heart where resides all goodness and sin.

Second, His teaching fulfilled the law. He taught universal, absolute truth and goodness that elevated Old Testament principles to a higher plane. Jesus fulfilled the law in His teaching by showing the truth of the commands and separating them from the perversities imposed on the law by the religious leaders. His teaching fulfilled the law by taking areas prone to ethical manipulation and replacing them with absolute standards of truth and righteousness.

Christ's fulfillment of the law retained everything in the Old Testament, "which are written about Me in the Law of Moses and the Prophets and the Psalms" (Luke 24:44) that had permanent value and validity. He taught that everything in the Old Testament scheme had a part in the plan leading to fulfillment. All Old Testament principles that had moral or religious significance are still in existence in the teaching of Jesus. He fulfills the Old Testament by adding the highest ideals of the faith to the law as well as accomplishing the prophecies.

The fulfillment process is like apple fruit replacing an apple blossom. It has always been an apple tree and will always be an apple tree, but its appearance and usefulness is much improved. The new apple fruit comes out of the old blossom in a regular, naturally occurring process. The gospel, coming out of the Old Testament, does the same. "In that process what is unessential falls away of its own accord, while all that is essential and permanently useful is taken up into Christianity, more completely developed and applied, and reinforced by higher motives on the plane of broader principles."[10]

"Jesus, who appeared in the fullness of times, is the fulfiller of law and prophecy."[11] Jewish religionists expected the Messiah to dignify

---

10 Stevens, 9-16.
11 Franz Delitzsch, *Old Testament History of Redemption.* trans. Samuel I. Curtis. Edinburgh: T.& T. Clark; reprint 1988, (Peabody, MA: Hendrickson Publishers, 1881), 181.

the law and fulfill the prophets. That is exactly what He did, but not in a manner that coincided with their traditions and expectations of a secular kingdom. "He fulfilled the Law by dying on the cross and thereby satisfying forever the demands of the Laws against those who would believe on Him."[12]

Note that Christ states the law, as well as the prophets, tells of the coming Messiah: "For all the prophets and the Law prophesied until John" (Matt. 11:13). Moses gave the law long ago; there had been no prophets for four hundred years before John. John was the last Old Testament prophet so there would be nothing more to add concerning the Messiah. John differed only slightly from all the other Old Testament prophets. They prophesied concerning the coming kingdom. John preached that the kingdom was at hand. Former prophecies of a promised Messiah moved from future to present when John said, "Behold the Lamb of God" (John 1:29)!

Our Lord Himself explained this on the Emmaus Road when He conversed with the two disciples. "Then he said unto them, 'O fools, and slow of heart to believe all that the prophets have spoken: Ought not Christ to have suffered these things, and to enter into his glory?' And beginning at Moses and all the prophets, he expounded unto them in all the Scriptures the things concerning himself" (Luke 24:25–27). He showed them the light of the Old Testament is in the law and the prophets, who spoke of His coming and His kingdom.

"Christ as an atoning sacrifice for sin was the grand object of the whole sacrificial code of Moses; his passion and death were the fulfillment of its great object and design. Separate this sacrificial death of Christ from the law and the law has no meaning."[13] The law, therefore, points to the work of Christ. The law shows that every sinner is under

---

12 James Montgomery Boice, *The Sermon on the Mount.* (Grand Rapids, MI: Baker Books, 1972), 79.
13 Adam Clarke, *Commentary on the Whole Bible.* (Tempe, AZ: The Crosswire Software and Bible Society, 1810/1825). Comments on Romans 10:4.

the law, and consequently under the curse. The gospel shows men how to avoid the curse.

Our Savior fulfilled the Law because He was perfect; He lived the Law with an active obedience that no other man could, obeying every jot and tittle. His work on Calvary, His suffering and death, fulfilled the Law completely and gave men the power to live in the spirit of the Law. Under the new covenant, every reading, interpretation, or application of the law is irrelevant unless viewed through the salvific work of the Lord Jesus Christ.

Christ fulfilled all the prophecy in the Law, the Prophets, and the Writings. His life, death, and resurrection made the Law perfect. All the types, shadows, and prophecies surrounding the tabernacle, the altar, laver, candlesticks, the Temple veil, Holy of Holies, the sacrifices, lives of the Old Testament characters, everything, Christ fulfilled on the cross. That is the reason for the cross. That is the only scriptural view of the cross.

THE HOLY SPIRIT FULFILLS THE LAW IN THE HEARTS OF BELIEVERS

The nature of sin is rebellion against God. The flesh in sinful rebellion dwells in men before salvation. After salvation, the Spirit dwells in men also. Its testimony is in their conscience, and its powerful operation is in the heart. At Creation, God made man in union with himself, and his heart was His temple. Adam sinned, the temple was defiled, and God abandoned it. Jesus Christ's sacrifice and the Holy Spirit coming into the heart cleansed the temple. Once again, the heart of man can be a habitation of God through the Spirit. Only when the heart is again the residence of the Holy Spirit is the soul free from the effects of sin.

The writer of Hebrews quotes Jeremiah 31:33. "But this is the covenant which I will make with the house of Israel after those days," declares the Lord, "I will put My law within them and on their heart I will write it; and I will be their God, and they shall be My people" (Heb. 8:10). The law is within us, not external as it was in the Old Testament. "The new covenant will not be a new law (the old law was still good, just not fulfilled), but it will produce a new heart—i.e., it will confer a new motivation to obey the law of God."[14]

Through the Holy Spirit, God writes the law in the hearts and minds of believers. Once God wrote His law on stone and gave it to Moses. Now He writes it in the hearts of His people, "written not with ink but with the Spirit of the living God, not on tablets of stone but on tablets of human hearts" (2 Cor. 3:3). He will open their eyes and enlighten their understanding. Believers will be able to see the true, full, spiritual meaning of the law. They shall inwardly experience whatever He has commanded. God will influence His people with all the principles of law, truth, and holiness. They will be fully enlightened to comprehend, believe, and obey the law. Christians who believe Christ Jesus is the sin offering who condemned sin in the flesh, and are justified by faith with the Holy Spirit dwelling within, have the fulfillment of the law in their heart. "It is because the law has been written in our minds and our hearts that we are anxious to fulfill it, and are enabled to do so."[15]

"Who also made us adequate *as* servants of a new covenant, not of the letter but of the Spirit; for the letter kills, but the Spirit gives life" (2 Cor. 3:6). The phrase *but of the spirit* points to the spiritual holiness that undergirds the Mosaic Law. The new covenant, the gospel of the Lord Jesus Christ, brings the spiritual holiness of the law to light. With the gospel there is "a new power of obedience imparted, namely, the Holy Spirit."[16] "But now we have been released from the Law, having died to that by which we were bound, so that we serve in newness of

---

14 John F. Graybill, *Jeremiah in The Wycliffe Bible Commentary*, ed. Charles F. Pfeiffer and Everett F. Harrison. (Nashville: The Southwestern Co., 1962), 679.

15 D. Martyn Lloyd-Jones, *Studies in the Sermon on the Mount.* (Grand Rapids, MI: William B. Eerdmans Publishing Company, 1976), 169.

16 Robert Jamieson, A.R. Fausset, David Brown, *Commentary: Practical and Explanatory on the Whole Bible*, new and rev. ed. (Grand Rapids, Michigan: Zondervan, 1961), 899.

the Spirit and not in oldness of the letter" (Rom. 7:6). Living by the Mosaic Law was too difficult; even when men wanted to obey, they could not. The Holy Spirit dwelling in the heart of believers gives them the power to obey. The Holy Spirit leads Christians to a life that is greater than the sin nature the law exposes.

SALVATION IS BY FAITH IN BOTH TESTAMENTS

The law condemns sin and prescribes the only punishment for sin—death. Christ fulfilled the law on Calvary by taking all mankind's punishment for sin. God does not decide to overlook some sins so that men can enter heaven. That is against His holy character. Death is the only punishment for sin. That is why the law and prophets foretold of a Messiah who would die for our sin, all sin, all the sin of all men. His dying for us is the true fulfillment of the law because in the sinless, holy, spotless, blameless body of the Lord Jesus Christ, God punished sin forever.

The way of salvation revealed in the Old Testament was by grace, not obtained by works but by faith. It is not from human merit but on the merits of Christ's sacrificial work yet to come.

Now there is a clear continuity between the Testaments. God's righteousness (His saving act) is now visible outside the boundaries of the Old Testament covenant, which looked forward to this through the law and the prophets. God saves sinners by faith as shown in the gospel because He is merciful. He saves them when they repent and trust in the death and resurrection of Christ Jesus without the deeds of the law. Claiming any obedience to the law has no part in the justification of sinners. Evidently, that is what God intended from the beginning for it is "witnessed by the Law and the Prophets." Thus, the rites and ceremonies of the law and the preaching and predictions of the prophets that bear testimony to God's great plan of the ages are now fully disclosed. The law and the prophets unquestionably show how necessary it was for the Lord Jesus Christ to die for the salvation of man.

Our salvation fulfills the law in the pardoning of our guilt through the merit of Christ's sacrifice and the power of His grace. The law could aggravate our sinful nature into action, but it could not secure its own fulfillment. "For what the Law could not do, weak as it was through the flesh, God *did*: sending His own Son in the likeness of sinful flesh and *as an offering* for sin, He condemned sin in the flesh, so that the requirement of the Law might be fulfilled in us, who do not walk according to the flesh but according to the Spirit" (Romans 8:3-4). *Fulfilled* in this passage indicates the law is realized in believers. Christians are righteous because Christ took their place as a sinner perfectly fulfilling and satisfying the righteous demands of the law.

In 2 Corinthians 3:13-14, Paul relates the story found in Exodus 34:33 where Moses' face shone so brightly from the reflected glory of God that the people could not stand to look at him. Symbolically, Paul explained that the children of Israel were so spiritually blind that they could not see the final end of the Law and the hope it portended for Israel's future. That was how it was before Christ's ministry, and it was especially so to those who remained in Judaism after the resurrection of the Messiah and the preaching of His gospel. Spiritually, the veil covered their minds so their hearts were hardened and they could not see truth of the Gospel that fulfilled the Law. Paul writes here that the light and revelation of Christ removed the veil. There is a time coming when this veil will be no more and the body of that people shall turn to the Lord. When they do, they will finally grasp what Jesus said in Matthew 5:17, "Do not think that I came to abolish the Law or the Prophets; I did not come to abolish but to fulfill." John Calvin said:

> "When the Lord declares, that he came not to destroy the Law, but to fulfill; that until heaven and earth pass away, not one jot or tittle shall remain unfulfilled; he shows that his advent was not to derogate, in any degree, from the observance of the Law. And justly, since the very end of his coming was to remedy the transgression of the Law. Therefore, the doctrine of the Law has not been infringed by Christ, but remains,

that, by teaching, admonishing, rebuking, and correcting, it may fit and prepare us for every good work."[17]

The gospel frees men from the law of sin and death. The law is no longer an instrument for God's people to obey. Believers are not subject to live in obedience to the law in the same manner as the Old Testament Jews. "Yet, it remains as part of Scripture, and as such it is profitable for us because it bears witness to our Lord and Savior."[18] Nevertheless, obedience is an essential aspect of saving faith. John wrote: "For this is the love of God, that we keep His commandments; and His commandments are not burdensome" (1 John 5:3). Christ said, "If you love Me, you will keep My commandments" (John 14:15). Christ fulfilled the law. By being in Christ, we fulfill the law as we obey Him. The Mosaic Law is profitable because it supplies a righteous code of living that, when men follow, God is pleased. Christ's work brings believers into the state of true righteousness, which the law requires.

---

17 John Calvin, Institutes, 2.7.14.
18 Alva J. McClain, Law and Grace. 1954. Reprint, (Chicago: Moody Press, 1967), 58.

CHAPTER 9

THE TEN COMMANDMENTS

THE TEN COMMANDMENTS ARE AN integral part of the Judeo-Christian system. Christians as well as many non-believers consider the Ten Commandments to be sacrosanct. They feel this way even when they cannot name them in order or even remember all ten. People who make no pretense to obey them will argue passionately in their defense. As such, together with the common Bible stories, they are one of the few things people know about the Old Testament. For some, it is almost all they know of Christianity.

Affection for the Ten Commandments crosses theological boundaries. Scholars who contend the Mosaic Law is not for the Church Age will confidently declare the value and efficacy of the Ten Commandments. One theologian narrowed the usefulness of the Old Testament to just nineteen verses. He confidently declared that only the Ten Commandments and the two great commands are for Christians. "You shall love the Lord your God with all your heart and with all your soul and with all your might" (Deut. 6:5). "You shall not take vengeance, nor bear any grudge against the sons of your people, but you shall love your neighbor as yourself; I am the Lord" (Lev. 19:18).

Fee and Stuart write, "No other specific Old Testament laws can be proved to be strictly binding on Christians, valuable as it is for Christians to know all of the laws."[1] They justify their position with John 7:23, which says, "If a man receives circumcision on *the* Sabbath

---

1 Gordon Fee, Douglas Stuart, *How to Read the Bible for all Its Worth.* 3rd ed. (Grand Rapids, MI: Zondervan, 2003), 169.

so that the Law of Moses will not be broken, are you angry with Me because I made an entire man well on *the* Sabbath." It is a poor argument. Jesus was speaking of the hypocrisy of the Jews who would perform a circumcision on the Sabbath, but criticize Jesus for healing on the Sabbath.

Their position has obvious flaws. Consider Leviticus 19:14, which says, "You shall not curse a deaf man, nor place a stumbling block before the blind, but you shall revere your God; I am the Lord" is still binding. What Christian could countenance such behavior? Throughout the law are numerous other injunctions Christians would readily find compatible and binding in the Church Age.

DEATH PENALTY

Before looking at the Ten Commandments, it is necessary to discuss the death penalty, for it plays a significant role as a punishment for breaking the Mosaic Law.

God instituted the death penalty for murder after the Great Flood some 500 years before the law. "Whoever sheds man's blood, by man his blood shall be shed, for in the image of God He made man" (Gen. 9:6). Before the Flood, murder was not a capital crime. Because the shedding of blood was the instrument of salvation, God could not allow man to shed blood indiscriminately. Capital punishment has nothing to do with being a deterrent to crime. Human life is precious because God made man in His image. Man is special to God, and to have the temerity to murder another is an insult to the God who created man.

God expanded the number of capital offenses in the law to cover witchcraft, immorality, disobedience to parents, and flagrant disbelief and disregard for God. Paul called the law a "ministry of death, in letters engraved on stones" (2 Cor. 3:7) because the penalty for breaking the first eight commandments, as well as committing many other offenses, was death.

Death was not the penalty for lying, unless someone lied to authorities by falsely accusing someone of a capital crime, which led to their execution. In that case, the lie led to murder, and therefore the liar suffered the death penalty. In many instances, the sins of lying and covetousness will lead to violating one of the other commandments, and then death was the punishment.

Many people who hold the Ten Commandments in such high esteem have no idea the punishment for breaking most of them is death. Fortunately, under the gospel, God no longer enforces the spiritual and moral imperatives in the law by a death sentence. Instead, the same commands as found in the New Testament remind the believer of his union with Christ and the indwelling by the Holy Spirit.

The headings that follow are from the King James Version because they are the most familiar renderings of the Ten Commandments.

1. THOU SHALT HAVE NO OTHER GODS BEFORE ME (EXOD. 20:3).

Moses writes the death penalty for having other gods a few chapters later. "He who sacrifices to any god, other than to the Lord alone, shall be utterly destroyed" (Exod. 22:20).

The New Testament does not repeat this command. The principle that men should only worship the Triune God is confirmed, "For there is one God, *and* one mediator also between God and men, *the* man Christ Jesus" (1 Tim. 2:5). Once Christ fulfilled the law, nowhere in the New Testament is the death penalty for not worshipping only God the Creator repeated. The sins of men offend God. In fulfilling the law, Jesus Christ, being both God and man, mediates between men and God.

The penalty of the "first commandment has been annulled, but the moral principle that only the true God should be worshipped and served abides forever."[2] Paul, in restraining the crowd at Lystra who

---

2 Roy L. Aldridge, The Mosaic Ten Commandments Compared to their Restatements in the New Testament. *Bibliotheca Sacra.* July 1961, 251.

wanted to worship him and Barnabas as gods, declared, "Men, why are you doing these things? We are also men of the same nature as you, and preach the gospel to you that you should turn from these vain things to a living God, who made the heaven and the earth and the sea and all that is in them" (Acts 14:15).

Ultimately, there is a penalty. Wicked men who refuse to repent and accept Christ as their Savior do face a death penalty—eternal damnation, "For the wages of sin is death" (Rom. 6:23) for those who reject Christ.

2. THOU SHALT NOT MAKE UNTO THEE ANY GRAVEN IMAGE (EXOD. 20:4).

After Aaron led the nation into sin with the golden calf, God used the death penalty to punish the idolaters. He instructed Moses, "Thus says the Lord, the God of Israel, 'Every man *of you* put his sword upon his thigh, and go back and forth from gate to gate in the camp, and kill every man his brother, and every man his friend, and every man his neighbor.' So the sons of Levi did as Moses instructed, and about three thousand men of the people fell that day" (Exod. 32:27–28).

The Jerusalem Council decreed that believers "abstain from things contaminated by idols" (Acts 15:20). It is still wrong to worship idols, but Christ's fulfillment of the law lessened the penalty. Paul reminds his readers to avoid idol worship, but meat sacrificed to idols in pagan worship services and later sold in the meat market is acceptable if it does not bother the conscience (1 Cor. 10:25). He warns the Corinthians several times, "You know that when you were pagans, *you were* led astray to the mute idols, however you were led" (1 Cor. 12:2). "Do not be idolaters, as some of them were" (1 Cor. 10:7). "Therefore, my beloved, flee from idolatry" (1 Cor. 10:14). Later he points out how bonds with unbelievers in worship are wrong, "What agreement has the temple of God with idols? For we are the temple of the living God; just as God said" (2 Cor. 6:16).

John warned, "Little children, guard yourselves from idols" (1 John 5:21). This passage describes the relationship between the believer and the Lord Jesus Christ. Mercy and forgiveness of sin are possible because Christ fulfilled the law. The law as written in the Decalogue and the death penalty are not in effect, but the principle is valid and expanded to include anything that comes between a believer and Christ. God's people are to keep themselves from every inward idol and personal desire that takes the place of true worship or separates them from God. The indwelling Holy Spirit prompts Christians to avoid idolatry.

The primary worship and learning principle taught in the New Testament is that God has "willed that his church be instructed, not by dumb images, but by the preaching of His Word."[3]

3. THOU SHALT NOT TAKE THE NAME OF THE LORD THY GOD IN VAIN (EXOD. 20:7).

God's name is precious. The penalty for men who blaspheme His name is death. "You shall speak to the sons of Israel, saying, if anyone curses his God, then he will bear his sin. Moreover, the one who blasphemes the name of the Lord shall surely be put to death; all the congregation shall certainly stone him. The alien as well as the native, when he blasphemes the Name, shall be put to death" (Lev. 24:15–16). Note this injunction is for non-Israelites as well as the chosen people.

There is no death penalty for profanity and blasphemy against the name of God in the New Testament. Numerous references to careful speech indicate that everything a believer says must be with the glorious holiness of God in mind.

Oaths and Vows

The Old Testament instructs Israelites to honor any vow they make. "If a man makes a vow to the Lord, or takes an oath to bind himself

---

3 Charles Hodge, *Systematic Theology. Vol. 3*, (Peabody, MA: Hendrickson Publishers, 2008), 304.

with a binding obligation, he shall not violate his word; he shall do according to all that proceeds out of his mouth" (Num. 30:2). The law permitted oaths made unto the Lord. It would appear Jesus negates this in Matthew 5:34, "But I say to you, make no oath at all, either by heaven, for it is the throne of God." This is not the case. The Jews had formed a custom of swearing on anything but God. They had wrongly determined that an oath to anything other than to God was not binding. Therefore, they created many oaths to suit their purposes, give weight to their words and promises, but if they broke them, it would not matter because the vow was not to God.

Jesus called out this evil practice of lying curses. He certainly did not intend to abolish those instances, which Moses allowed, and in some instances required the administration of an oath (Exod. 22:11, Num. 5:19). Note that God swore by Himself (Gen. 22:16-17, Heb. 6:13, 7:21). Jesus answered under oath before the Sanhedrin (Matt. 26:63), and Paul made an oath to the Corinthian church (2 Cor. 1:23). Even an angel swore unto God (Rev. 10:6). Jesus was warning them, "You shall not make false vows, but shall fulfill your vows to the Lord" (Matt. 5:33). "We conclude, then, that judicial oaths, and oaths taken in the name of God on occasions of solemn religious importance, are not included in the prohibition. But as these are the only exceptions found in Scriptures, we conclude that all other oaths are forbidden. Looking at the details of the paragraph, we find that oaths by heaven and by the earth, by Jerusalem and by the head, are utterly meaningless save as they have reference to God."[4] Thus the Mosaic edict is still valid, "You shall not swear falsely by My name, so as to profane the name of your God; I am the Lord" (Lev. 19:12). A merciful God does not require the death penalty in this era of fulfilled law. Forgiveness is available for men if they repent for committing this sin.

---

4 J. W. McGarvey. and Philip Y. Pendleton, *The Fourfold Gospel and Commentary on Acts of Apostles*. (Tempe, AZ: The Crosswire Software and Bible Society, 1863, 1882).

4. REMEMBER THE SABBATH DAY, TO KEEP IT HOLY (EXOD. 20:8).

The seventh day Sabbath versus Sunday worship is a source of contention for some believers and a source of confusion for even more.

Once again, there is an example of the death penalty for breaking the Sabbath. A man was found gathering wood on the Sabbath, and he was brought to Moses to determine what to do with him. "Then the Lord said to Moses, 'The man shall surely be put to death; all the congregation shall stone him with stones outside the camp'" (Num. 15:35).

The Pharisees corrupted the idea of the seventh day Sabbath beyond recognition as a day of rest. They added a list of restrictive rules that essentially led to a near complete cessation of activity. So many rules had evolved covering nearly every activity of man that the day was no longer restful but instead a burden filled with pitfalls for the theologically unwary. Paul warned the Colossians not to fall into that quagmire (Col. 2:16). The early church heeded his words, for the first three centuries of the Christian era; worship on the first day of the week was never confounded with the seventh day Sabbath. Present day confusion of the Jewish and Christian institutions is due to a turning aside from apostolic teaching. They have lost the truth that Jesus preached, "The Sabbath was made for man, and not man for the Sabbath" (Mark 2:27).

Sabbath is an intermission, meaning to rest from labor. Throughout the Old Testament God directed the observance of Sabbaths at the beginning or end of Jewish festivals. Israel was to humble themselves and not work on the Day of Atonement. That day was not the seventh day of the week, but the tenth day of the seventh month (Lev. 16:29). The tenth of the month can fall on any day of the week. Yet, that day is called a Sabbath (Lev. 16:31). Thus, a Sabbath is a day of rest and worship, but not always observed on the seventh day of the week.

God instituted the Sabbath at Creation. It is not part of the Mosaic Law. The principles contained in the Sabbath are valid for all time, and God saw fit to reemphasize the Sabbath in the law. First, it is beneficial for men to take time to rest and recuperate from their labor. Second, all men need to stop their worldly pursuits and reflect on God. As their Creator, He fashioned men with a need to spend one-seventh of their time with their thoughts turned toward Him.

Christ fulfilled all the laws regarding the Sabbath. In the Church Age, the Sabbath or the Lord's Day is the first day of the week. Two New Testament passages support this change. "And upon the first *day* of the week, when the disciples came together to break bread, Paul preached unto them, ready to depart on the morrow; and continued his speech until midnight" (Acts 20:7 KJV). "On the first day of every week each one of you is to put aside and save, as he may prosper, so that no collections be made when I come" (1 Cor. 16:2 KJV). The first day of the week became the Lord's Day, the day Christians meet for worship, in which they commemorate the resurrection of our Lord. Among Christians, the first day of the week took the place of the Jewish seventh day of rest.

The New Testament principle is that men ought to set aside some time for worship of the God who created them, the Son who saved them, and the Spirit who dwells within. "Neither the Jewish Sabbath nor the Lord's Day were ever intended to detract from the broader spiritual truth that all of the believer's time and service belong to God (Rom. 12:1–2)."[5]

5. HONOR THY FATHER AND MOTHER (EXOD. 20:12).

The death penalty for dishonoring parents is clear. "He who strikes his father or his mother shall surely be put to death" (Exod. 21:15). "He who curses his father or his mother shall surely be put to

---

5 Aldridge, 251-258.

death" (Exod. 21:17). "A rebellious son was to be stoned to death by the elders" (Deut. 21:18–21).

In Matthew 15:3–4, Jesus cited the law, "And He answered and said to them, 'Why do you yourselves transgress the commandment of God for the sake of your tradition? For God said, "honor your father and mother," and, "he who speaks evil of father or mother is to be put to death."'" Some consider this verse as justification for Christians to observe the Old Testament law. However, that is out of context. Jesus was scolding the Pharisees for transgressing the law. Using this verse to justify observing the law is fallacious since the Old Testament economy was still in effect during the time Jesus was alive and would remain so until the resurrection. Christ lived under the Mosaic Law and encouraged its observance. Only after his death and resurrection did Christ fulfill the law.

This command appears twice in the New Testament. Neither has the death penalty attached. "Children, obey your parents in the Lord, for this is right. Honor your father and mother (which is the first commandment with a promise), so that it may be well with you, and that you may live long on the earth" (Eph. 6:1–3). Old Testament children who obeyed the fifth commandment had a promise of a long life in the land of Palestine. In the New Testament, the promise is for a long life on earth.

The second is "Children, be obedient to your parents in all things, for this is well-pleasing to the Lord" (Col. 3:20). The idea of pleasing the Lord illustrates how Christ's fulfillment of the law takes the commandment to a much higher plane of spiritual living. The principle of respect and honor to parents upon which the law rides is as timeless as the holiness of God and applies to all believers in all ages. Only when men bow before the sovereign authority of God will they be able to keep the command to honor father and mother.[6]

---

6 R. Brainsma, The Third Use of the Law. *Standard Bearer*. October 15, 2002, 39.

6. THOU SHALT NOT KILL (EXOD. 20:13).

Mosaic Law is clear. "He who strikes a man so that he dies shall surely be put to death" (Exod. 21:12). Provisions for accidental death and manslaughter were part of the law, but those who committed premeditated murder faced execution.

Like the Sabbath, God instituted the death penalty for murder long before the law. God included it with one of the four injunctions He gave Noah after the Flood: "Whoever sheds man's blood, by man his blood shall be shed, for in the image of God He made man" (Gen. 9:6).

Under the law, only the physical act of committing murder was punishable. In the New Testament, murder is much more than the actual taking of a life. "Everyone who hates his brother is a murderer; and you know that no murderer has eternal life abiding in him" (1 John 3:15). Hatred in the heart is the same attitude that leads to the action. Christianity forbids believers from harboring hatred in their hearts. Hatred is murder not yet committed. Fulfillment of the law includes not only actions but also the attitude of the heart.

7. THOU SHALT NOT COMMIT ADULTERY (EXOD. 20:14).

The death penalty for adultery is unequivocal. "If *there is* a man who commits adultery with another man's wife, one who commits adultery with his friend's wife, the adulterer and the adulteress shall surely be put to death" (Lev. 20:10).

Like murder, the heart attitude with this sin is significant in the New Testament. Lustful desires are incipient adultery. "You have heard that it was said, you shall not commit adultery; but I say to you that everyone who looks at a woman with lust for her has already committed adultery with her in his heart" (Matt. 5:27-28). The commandment prevented the act; now the prohibition extends to lust. "So the Spirituality of the law is seen in that it deals with the attitudes as well as actions."[7] The New Testament explains in detail what constitutes adultery.

Love in a marriage between husband and wife is like Christ's love for the church. That comparison ought to give all believers pause before they do anything to violate the sanctity of the relationship. It is unconscionable to imagine Christ betraying His church. So spouses ought to feel toward each other. Under the gospel, no moral impurity is acceptable. "Flee immorality. Every *other* sin that a man commits is outside the body, but the immoral man sins against his own body. Or do you not know that your body is a temple of the Holy Spirit who is in you, whom you have from God, and that you are not your own" (1 Cor. 6:18–19). Thus, the fulfillment of this command is much more than the physical act, but includes all manner of lustful and immoral thoughts. When Christians know and experience the inseparable bond that unites Christ and His bride, the church, honoring the marriage vows becomes a way of life.

8. THOU SHALT NOT STEAL (EXOD. 20:15).

Typically, stealing property under the Mosaic Law required restitution, usually by an amount greater than what was taken. One theft, kidnapping (stealing a man), was punishable by death: "He who kidnaps a man, whether he sells him or he is found in his possession, shall surely be put to death" (Exod. 21:16).

Under the Gospel, the approach to preventing theft is dramatically different and magnificently illustrates the principle of grace. "He who steals must steal no longer; but rather he must labor, performing with his own hands what is good, so that he will have *something* to share with one who has need" (Eph. 4:28). Converted thieves work at legitimate labor in order to give to the needy to help remove their temptation to steal. Christ fulfilling the law

---

7 Harold Vaughn, An Unscriptural Division. *The Baptist Examiner.* June 11, 1998, 1, 8, 9.

transforms stealing into the principle of stewardship. "A Christian is stealing if he is not a good giver."[8]

9. THOU SHALT NOT BEAR FALSE WITNESS (EXOD. 20:16).

The Jews had turned the command "Thou shalt not lie" into an instrument of untruthfulness. Extra-biblical rules permitted them to get away with just about anything. Their words were treacherous, violating the idea that a man's word was his bond. "Let your word be enough. Esteem that to be as binding as if you had coupled your statement with Jehovah's name."[9]

God hates lying, and He will destroy all liars. "You destroy those who speak falsehood; the Lord abhors the man of bloodshed and deceit" (Psa. 5:6). Similarly, "But You, O God, will bring them down to the pit of destruction; men of bloodshed and deceit will not live out half their days" (Psa. 55:23). God detests lying. Numerous similar passages describe how God's distaste for liars will lead to their destruction. They will be cut off, destroyed, their mouths will be stopped, they shall not be unpunished, nor will they escape.

The concept that God will punish liars continues into the New Testament, "But for the cowardly and unbelieving and abominable and murderers and immoral persons and sorcerers and idolaters and all liars, their part *will be* in the lake that burns with fire and brimstone, which is the second death" (Rev. 21:8). Only God consigns condemned sinners to the lake of fire.

Since the fulfillment of the law, truthfulness becomes an essential part of the character of a Christian. In that respect God's people must never lie, must always tell the truth. "Do not lie to one another, since you laid aside the old self with its *evil* practices, and have put on the

8 Aldridge, 256.
9 George B. Stevens, Gospel and Law in the Teaching of Jesus Christ. *Searching Together*, Spring/Autumn 1992, 9-16.

new self who is being renewed to a true knowledge according to the image of the One who created him" (Col. 3:9–10).

Human courts do not institute the death penalty for lying except when it is part of another crime. In each of the many passages that reveal God's hatred for lying, the punishment will come from the hand of God. In no instance is there a provision for the administration of judicial punishment for lying unless the lying is part of some other crime.

Lying is a universal sin that exists everywhere. Christians are to abandon not just lying but all the things they did before salvation that conflict with the gospel of the Lord Jesus Christ. "That, in reference to your former manner of life, you lay aside the old self, which is being corrupted in accordance with the lusts of deceit" (Eph. 4:22).

10. THOU SHALT NOT COVET (EXOD. 20:17).

The Mosaic Law states no penalty for covetousness in thought only. If the sin leads to murder, adultery, theft, or some other violation, then the death penalty would apply as the indirect punishment for the sin of covetousness.

Once again, the fulfillment of the law takes this sin to a higher spiritual plane. In Jesus' words, "Then He said to them, 'Beware, and be on your guard against every form of greed; for not *even* when one has an abundance does his life consist of his possessions'" (Luke 12:15).

As the covetous man never has enough of wealth, the appetite for material gain increases in proportion to its indulgence. Covetousness is the love of gain. Linked to it are the related sins of greed, murder, lying, fornication, and adultery. Lying is an abomination in the sight of God.

Scripture equates covetousness with idolatry. "For this you know with certainty, that no immoral or impure person or covetous man, who is an idolater, has an inheritance in the kingdom of Christ and God" (Eph. 5:5). Covetousness is worship of the creature instead of the

Creator, the highest treason against the King of kings, which is like idolatry of self.

Paul describes how to deal with the sin of covetousness, "Not that I speak from want, for I have learned to be content in whatever circumstances I am" (Phil. 4:11).

TEN COMMANDMENTS FULFILLED

Because of great fondness for the Ten Commandments, many Christians believe obedience to them is essential. Obviously, this creates a problem because no modern legal system will allow strict adherence to them. Stevens explains the way to apply them in the Church Age: "The essential substance of the Ten Commandments consists of changeless principles of righteousness, and is therefore a part of Christianity. In that sense, the Christian is under the Ten Commandments."[10]

None of the Ten Commandments is in the New Testament with the same force and penalties of Mosaic legislation. All the moral principles of the commandments do appear in the New Testament, but in a framework of grace. The Christian "is under the eternal moral law of God, which demands far more than the Ten Commandments. It calls for nothing less than conformity to the character of God."[11]

Christ fulfilled all of the Ten Commandments. That does not mean He abolished them. All ten are still applicable in the New Testament, but each has undergone some degree of modification through fulfillment. Children should still obey their parents, but for a different reason. In the Old Testament, they obeyed to obtain long life in the Promised Land. In the New Testament, they obey so "that it may be well with you, and that you may live long on the earth" (Eph. 6:3). There is still a day set aside to worship, but on resurrection day, not the seventh day.

---

10 Stevens, 9-16.
11 Aldridge, 251.

When the veil covering the Holy of Holies tore from top to bottom, Christ established a new way. "By a new and living way which He inaugurated for us through the veil, that is, His flesh" (Heb. 10:20). Formerly, only the high priest could pass through the veil to atone for the sins of the people. In this new way, all believers "have access to the heavenly Holy of Holies, that is, to God's presence in heaven itself, through the flesh of Christ offered as our propitiatory sacrifice for sin."[12] He fulfilled the law, thus meeting the standards of the law for lost humanity. In doing so, He satisfied both the precept and penalty of the law. His broken body and shed blood atoned for our sins. "God has forever removed the barrier which stood between mankind and Himself."[13] The legal age is terminated!

The Mosaic Law was a code of legislation with exacting and severe penalties for every violation. Under the Gospel, the same moral principles exist, but Christ, in fulfilling the law, supplied His people with grace. Therefore, a committed Christian will not hesitate to obey the Ten Commandments because he knows they are, in their fulfilled state, God's divine will for him in this life. Because he loves God, he has a desire to do the will of God.

Because Christ fulfilled the law, the Spirit-filled Christian is capable of discernment and recognition, and has greater participation in a better relationship between God and man. Because man is capable of full knowledge concerning his new relationship, he is powerfully influenced by the Savior who made him.

The moral principle of worship and service is to the true God only. The Old Testament principle behind the law remains in this era. The Ten Commandments, along with the entire law, still have validity in the Church Age, but with a difference. Instead of civil government exacting the penalty for breaking the law, the New Testament expands

---

12 Comments on Hebrews 10:20. Family Bible Notes from the Nazarene Users Group. (Tempe, AZ: The Crosswire Software and Bible Society).

13 G. G. Findlay, Colossians in *The Pulpit Commentary*, ed. H.D.M. Spence & Joseph Exell. (New York: Funk & Wagnalls, 1913), 89.

the concept or principle of the commandments. Obedience to the Decalogue is on a higher spiritual plane because of grace and the power Christians have with the indwelling of the Holy Spirit.

The prophet Micah summarizes the use of the commandments of God with these words in which no true Church Age believer can find fault: "He has told you, O man, what is good; and what does the Lord require of you but to do justice, to love kindness, and to walk humbly with your God" (Micah 6:8). The "good" is the good and wonderful things to come with the Messiah, of which the law is a shadow. The "good" is what believers should aim for. The "good" is where a Christian's true happiness rests. The "good" is more than the future state of happiness in eternity, but the source of all present joy and contentment. The Ten Commandments are good because they prepared the way for the gospel.

CHAPTER 10

LAW VERSUS GRACE

THE TITLE OF THIS CHAPTER is a misnomer. It is accurate, however, in that it reflects the confusion permeating Christendom on this topic. Grace and Law are not the same, but neither are they in conflict. Far too many believers view the question as either/or. Indeed, the situation has progressed to the point that some Christians discount the Old Testament completely and some pastors will not preach from it. Yet others place heavy emphasis on some point of law as necessary. The Lord Jesus Christ fulfilled the law, grace completes the law, and they fit together perfectly.

LAW DEFINED

This book has already defined Law in detail.[1] The law could not save mankind or give life because it is impossible. That was not its purpose.

God introduced the law to the Israelites because of sin to point the way to redemption. "Why the Law then? It was added because of transgressions, having been ordained through angels by the agency of a mediator, until the seed would come to whom the promise had been made" (Gal. 3:19). The law revealed God's true character and the "exceeding sinfulness of sin."[2] Its purpose is to regulate the conduct of men. Even though "holy, righteous, and good" (Rom. 7:12), the law

---

1 See Chapter Four, The Purpose of the Law.
2 From the title of a book by the Puritan and Congregationalist preacher, Jeremiah Burroughs (1599-1646). *The Evil of Evils: The Exceeding Sinfulness of Sin.*

cannot justify the souls of men. It cannot pardon sin. It cannot purify the heart. It can only condemn sinners to death.

An honest comparison of the law to how humanity lives will reveal the horrific excess and rampant sin that permeates the very existence of everyone living. The law shows sinful men they are unable to justify themselves before God. The law teaches men their need for salvation in the Lord Jesus Christ. That is why Paul called the law "our tutor *to lead us* to Christ" (Gal. 3:24).

GRACE DEFINED

Theologians have identified two kinds of grace. One is common grace, which is God's goodness to a sin-wracked world. Common grace is a restraint upon the excesses of sin that would properly require immediate execution of wrath. Common grace is viewed as every favor and blessing of God of a general nature that does not include salvation. God is good and merciful to the lost as well as the Christian. "For He causes His sun to rise on *the* evil and the good, and sends rain on *the* righteous and *the* unrighteous" (Matt. 5:45).

Special grace is the working of God to the elect that provides for their salvation due to the act of redemption by Christ on Calvary. This chapter concerns itself with special grace.

Grace makes salvation possible. Grace is the manifestation of God's goodness to men, frequently described as unmerited favor from God toward men. Specifically, "It is undeserved favor bestowed upon those who are positively deserving of the wrath of God."[3] There is nothing implied by the word to indicate the favor is deserved.

Grace is the mercy of God, as distinguished from His justice. Grace is also any benefits God in His mercy gives to believers, including divine love and pardon from sins. Grace is a state of acceptance with God and enjoyment of His divine favor.

---

3 Alan Cairns, ed., *Dictionary of Theological Terms.* 2nd ed. (Greenville, SC: Ambassador-Emerald International, 1998), 167.

God demonstrated grace in the Old Testament when He kept giving the Israelites chance after chance after chance to repent. Their continued refusal to repent proved they only deserved the same destruction with which He judged the heathen.

Grace is nearly an equivalent word for Christianity as a religion of dependence on God through Christ. The very idea of Christianity may be summed up as a gospel of grace: "But I do not consider my life of any account as dear to myself, so that I may finish my course and the ministry which I received from the Lord Jesus, to testify solemnly of the gospel of the grace of God" (Acts 20:24). Grace is the power of God for salvation to everyone that believes.

Grace is a fundamental characteristic of Christianity. The basic passage is the definition in Romans 11:6, which states, "But if it is by grace, it is no longer on the basis of works, otherwise grace is no longer grace." There are only two possible sources of salvation: men's works or God's grace. They are complete opposites. Since man cannot save himself, his works are of no value; salvation must come from God. Neither can salvation come from any combination of the two. Grace in this sense is an attitude on God's part that proceeds entirely from within Him. It has no dependence on any characteristic or behavior in men.

A single idea is actually present in almost every use of *grace* in Scripture. All a Christian has or is, rests exclusively in God and Christ, and depends utterly on God through Christ. The hope of eternity is for those who look to their Father in loving confidence for every benefit—pardon for sin or for the strength for daily living.

The power of the Holy Spirit enables believers to understand the spiritual import of the Mosaic Law. The original holiness as well as the spirit of the Law is still in effect, but now with God's grace we serve Him in true spiritual obedience with true spiritual meaning. Grace brings us from gross imperfection into a state of perfection and excellence. Justification, sanctification, pardon, holiness, and the

158 A BIBLICIST VIEW OF LAW AND GOSPEL

peace of God were impossible solely by the law. Yet, the grace of God makes them available to all mankind.

"The New Testament speaks generally of the grace of God as the determining factor in man's turning to God. Even that faith which is the condition of salvation is due to the grace of God. Everything, therefore, from first to last is by grace, whether of redemption or of sanctification."[4]

Grace is freely given. It empowers men for service and enables them to lead a successful Christian life. Saints are heirs of grace and under grace. They are what they are by grace. They abound in gifts of grace and should grow in grace.

Because salvation is not dependent upon keeping the law, Christians live under a covenant of grace. Nevertheless, living under grace does not release believers from observing the fulfilled law as a rule of proper Christian living.

The law is not opposed to grace; the two are compatible. The law, since Christ fulfilled it, laid the foundation for grace. The law is still in effect, but tempered by grace. "Every one of the moral commands in the Law is, in its true and ideal meaning, still binding."[5] That is true because Christ fulfilled the Law. He did not abolish it. By grace, the Holy Spirit puts the law in the hearts of Christians and enables them to live obediently.

ANTINOMIANISM

Antinomianism means against the law. The term applies to those who believe the moral aspects of the Mosaic Law are not binding upon believers in any sense as a rule and guide for Christian living. Antinomians contend the gospel is a perfect law of life and

---

4 Alan Richardson, *A Theological Wordbook of the Bible.* (New York: The MacMillan Company, 1950), 102.
5 A. Lukyn Williams, Matthew, vol. 1 in *The Pulpit Commentary*, ed. H.D.M. (Spence & Joseph Exell. New York: Funk & Wagnalls, 1913), 157.

righteousness, so there is no need for the Ten Commandments or Moses.

Antinomians abolish a portion of the Law, remove it, or simply disregard the entire Law as unimportant. The idea is that the gospel frees Christians from required obedience to any law, whether scriptural, civil, or moral. Its adherents contend that under the gospel dispensation of grace, the moral law is of no use or obligation because faith alone and the gift of divine grace is all that is necessary for salvation.

Extreme antinomians hold the view that Christians can sin without consequence because once saved, with sins forgiven, they believe the grace of God prevents them from ever sinning again. No matter what they do wrong, it will not matter. "Do we then nullify the Law through faith? May it never be! On the contrary, we establish the Law" (Rom. 3:31). "We must beware of Antinomianism; that is, of supposing that, because Christ has been obedient unto death, there is no necessity for our obedience to his righteous commandments. If this were so, the grace of Christ would tend to the destruction of the Law, and not to its establishment. He only is saved from his sins who has the law of God written in his heart; and he alone has the Law written in his heart who lives an innocent, holy, and useful life."[6]

Antinomians cite several verses to support their position. The passages they use actually mean the Law is not required for salvation. Instead, Christians are under grace with the imputation of Christ's perfect righteousness through faith without works. "A careful reading of the very texts antinomians use to support their view will show that they impose a meaning on the words of Scripture that the writers of Scripture never intended."[7] Understood in the context of the entire passage, these verses invalidate the heresy that Christians do not have to follow established moral laws found in both Testaments. They cannot rely only on faith and divine grace to live in a manner pleasing

---

6 Commentary on Romans 3:31. Adam Clarke, *Commentary on the Whole Bible.* (Tempe, AZ: The Crosswire Software and Bible Society, 1810/1825).
7 Cairns, 30.

to God. Four of the more common verses antinomians use to justify their incorrect position are explained here.

Galatians 2:19

> "For through the Law I died to the Law, so that I might live to God."

This verse when kept in context with the rest of the passage shows that, in Christ, believers are legally free from the law condemning them. Paul is explaining that through the law he is deeply convinced of his utter sinfulness and helplessness. The consequence of the nature of the law means he is dead to any hope or expectation of help or of salvation from the law. Since the law has no salvation, he must take refuge in the law of Jesus Christ. The gospel makes him dead to the law, and the gospel saves him from death, permitting him to live unto God.

Romans 6:14

> "For sin shall not be master over you, for you are not under law but under grace."

God delivered Christians from the law as a means of righteousness. Using this verse as a basis for antinomianism is foolish because of the very next verse. "What then? Shall we sin because we are not under law but under grace? May it never be" (Rom. 6:15)! Even though God saves by free grace, the righteous standard of the Law is a valid and useful rule of life. The grace of God teaches us spiritual principles. Grace is not an excuse to live anyway we want.

Romans 7:6

> "But now we have been released from the Law, having died to that by which we were bound, so that we serve in newness of the Spirit and not in oldness of the letter."

In the context of the surrounding verses, Paul is showing the Law is satisfied, not dead. Christians can say they have "died to that by which we were bound." They are free from the bondage of the law that condemned them to death because of their sin. They now serve God in spirit and in the true spiritual meaning.

1 Timothy 1:9

> "Realizing the fact that law is not made for a righteous person, but for those who are lawless and rebellious, for the ungodly and sinners, for the unholy and profane, for those who kill their fathers or mothers, for murderers."

The Greek word translated *is not made* has the idea of "to lie upon." What Paul is saying is the law lies upon sinners, not a righteous man who is justified.

Doctrine determines conduct, and the deviant sinful practices listed here are contrary to sound doctrine—in either Testament. The "lawless" are those who refuse to submit to any law. The "rebellious" are those who do not acknowledge authority and choose to live according to their selfish desires. The "ungodly" have no religion. They refuse to recognize God. "Sinners" are those who transgress the law. The "unholy" are unclean within and without. "Profane" men are so unholy and abominable they are not fit to attend any public worship. The unholy and profane violate the third and fourth commandments. "Murderers of fathers and murderers of mothers" denote the vilest of all crimes; that one would raise his hand against a parent. They break the fifth commandment. A "murderer" is one who violates the sixth commandment and kills another human. It is inconceivable that any antinomian can find fault with this use of the law in the Church Age.

Those with true obedience to God do not live believing they can sin all they want because a crucified Savior has already died for their sin and made them righteous. That thinking leads to an ungodly life-style without the power of God. The result is immorality, divorce, materialism, dishonesty, covetousness, and untold other sins, all which show an obvious deficit of love toward God and man.

The law shows what is contrary to sound doctrine and what is in agreement with the gospel. The gospel carries out the principles of the law. "Every one of the commands in the Law is, in its true and ideal meaning, still binding."[8] When walking in the Spirit, believers will always be in agreement with, but never in conflict with, the law.

Someone counted more than one hundred commands recorded in the New Testament. Christians must reject any system of theology that downplays the necessity of obeying these commands as heretical.

Fulfilled Law has Value

The New Testament makes obedience to God's law an indicator of a true believer: "By this we know that we have come to know Him, if we keep His commandments. The one who says, 'I have come to know Him,' and does not keep His commandments, is a liar, and the truth is not in him" (1 John 2:3–4).

Paul boldly declared, "For I joyfully concur with the law of God in the inner man" (Rom. 7:22).

The writer of Hebrews, quoting Jeremiah, said, "For this is the covenant that I will make with the house of Israel after those days, says the Lord: I will put My laws into their minds, and I will write them on their hearts. And I will be their God, and they shall be My people" (Heb. 8:10). This verse verifies the law is a useful rule for Christian living.

"Do we then nullify the Law through faith? May it never be! On the contrary, we establish the Law" (Rom. 3:31). In effect, Paul is asking, "Does the fact that God saves sinners through faith in Christ lessen the sanctity and authority of his law as an expression of his will, or the obligations of men to obey it?"[9] Paul is forcefully declaring it does not.

---

8 Williams, 157.

9 Commentary on Romans 3:31. Family Bible Notes from the Nazarene Users Group. (Tempe, AZ: The Crosswire Software and Bible Society).

It does just the opposite. Far from it, Paul continues, "we establish the law" to show its excellence and never-changing obligations. Believers establish the law so it can lead men to persevere in their attempts to be successfully obedient to it. The preaching of the gospel does not negate the moral requirements of the Law.

The gospel acknowledges we have a law. The gospel upholds the law in that there are legal penalties for sin. The gospel upholds the law because of what the law says about the lives of God's people.

Christians must beware of antinomianism. Never suppose that because Christ died for the sin of the human race, there is no need for obedience to the righteous Old Testament commands fulfilled in the New Testament. If obedience were unnecessary, then grace would tend to destroy the law instead of Jesus fulfilling it. When justified, the Holy Spirit writes the law of God in the believer's heart. The more Christians understand justification, the more they will value the law. The law is right in condemning men as sinners. Believers should value how Jesus Christ took their punishment under the law. If God's people love Him, they will also love and obey the law.

LEGALISM

A dictionary definition of legalism is "a strict, literal, or excessive conformity to the law." In theology, legalism is a strict adherence to the Law or a set of rules as a means of salvation. It can also be observance of the law or a set of rules seen as necessary to keep one's salvation.

Alva McClain calls legalism "a theological disaster, bringing and compounding confusion into our views of sin, of salvation of the work of Christ, and even of the doctrine of God."[10]

The term *legalism* has several variations; all are similar, and all are heretical. In one form or another, they reveal themselves as the opposite of antinomianism.

---

10 Alva McClain, *Law and Grace*. 1954. Reprint, (Chicago: Moody Press, 1967), 51.

One, is salvation is by works. Personal righteousness is enough for men to earn their place in heaven.

A second is *neonomianism*, which is a false idea that saving faith includes works of obedience. It often manifests itself as God calls, but faith is man's part in salvation. Doing good works is a condition of salvation instead of being the fruit of saving faith.

Third, legalism is like the error of the Galatian church where they preached faith plus keeping the law as a Jew as necessary to be acceptable to God. Typically, salvation by faith falls away, and salvation by works predominates. The danger is that a believer constantly examines his works to determine if they are good enough for God. This leads to a diminished role in the sacrifice of Christ on Calvary in a hopeless struggle to be good enough.

Adherents of the fourth view contend that Christians must carefully observe the Old Testament moral law as a standard of Christian obedience.

In that familiar passage from Ephesians 2:8-10, Paul permanently destroys legalism:

> [8] For by grace you have been saved through faith; and that not of yourselves, *it is* the gift of God;
>
> [9] not as a result of works, so that no one may boast.
>
> [10] For we are His workmanship, created in Christ Jesus for good works, which God prepared beforehand so that we would walk in them.

The phrase *not as a result of works* means a manmade effort. It clearly means that neither faith nor salvation is a result of any works ever done by man or that man can do. On his own, man can do nothing. The idea of the word *workmanship* is, literally, "a thing of His making." God does every bit of the spiritual creation of men. Men cannot attribute their salvation to any works or merit of their own. It is of God's free mercy, manifested through Christ.

Having believed by the power of the Holy Spirit, Christians receive the Holy Spirit of promise "with which ye have been sealed for [the] day of redemption" (Eph. 4:30, Darby). Salvation is in no sense something men do for themselves but is the free "gift of God." No man can boast of having manufactured his own salvation or even contributed anything toward it. Grace, without any respect to human worthiness, confers the glorious gift of salvation.

Men do not receive salvation for their good works. God saves so that they may perform good works to the glory of God and the benefit of man. "We are not saved by, but created unto, good works."[11] Works do not justify men, but justified men work for the Savior.

Adding legalistic works to the gospel destroys the gospel. Even the minutest detail added to the gospel takes away from the only way men can come to salvation. Paul warned the Galatians of the danger of legalistic salvation by works, explaining that man becomes "under obligation to keep the whole Law" (Gal. 5:3), which the Scripture proves many times is impossible.

I'M NOT UNDER LAW, I'M UNDER GRACE

Many Christians casually toss around the statement, "I'm not under law, I'm under grace." Sadly, many do so without fully understanding the implications of what they are saying.

The sentence poses doctrinal and theological difficulties. It implies the Law is of no effect in the Church Age. Since Christians do not practice the ceremonial law, they believe the Old Testament is not applicable. Nothing could be further from the truth; the shadows, types, and all they represent are still important. They claim the Old

---

11 Robert Jamieson, A. R. Fausset, David Brown, *Commentary: Practical and Explanatory on the Whole Bible*, new and rev. ed. (Grand Rapids, Michigan: Zondervan, 1961), 1284.

Testament is not valid, but they still argue for the supremacy of the Ten Commandments. They reject the Law as being for the Jews, yet teach their children Old Testament Bible stories. This confused faith is rooted in a poor understanding of the Law as well as the purpose of the Law.

Lack of Bible Knowledge

In many instances, it reveals antinomian tendencies they are unaware they possess. They view the work of Christ as having put an end to the Old Testament and its laws. They have no idea of what Christ meant in Matthew 5:17-18: "Do not think that I came to abolish the Law or the Prophets; I did not come to abolish but to fulfill. For truly I say to you, until heaven and earth pass away, not the smallest letter or stroke shall pass from the Law until all is accomplished." Such a skewed personal theology has its roots in poor Bible teaching. It would be unfair to ask them how they justify believing the Ten Commandments but not the rest of the Old Testament. Their Bible knowledge is so poor that many Christians have no idea where to find the Ten Commandments or any other important verse besides John 3:16.

A License to Sin

There is another, more sinister and wholly unbiblical meaning behind those words. Some Christians have the idea that being under grace permits them to sin with impunity because God forgave them at salvation. Tragically, some Christians believe that living according to biblical standards of separation is a matter of personal conviction. An activity is only wrong if the Christian thinks it is wrong, but it may be okay for others. Conversely, if they think it is right to do, then it is okay to do it.

This is not a new problem. In his epistle to the Romans, Paul wrote of Christians who felt it was acceptable to sin because, as believers, they would receive even more of God's grace. His response to that kind of thinking was emphatic. "What shall we say then? Shall we continue in sin, that grace may abound? God forbid. How shall we, that are dead to sin, live any longer therein" (Rom. 6:1–2)?

Christians living in sin often denounce fellow believers who uphold biblical standards as legalistic. They are usually the first to cry legalism when confronted with a biblical standard they do not want to obey. It is becoming far too common for a believer who takes a stand against some activity of life, even if found in the Bible, to be accused of legalism.

The cry of legalism[12] has become a pious sounding excuse by some to justify their sin and disobedience. In their defiance of God, they will declare, "I'm not convicted about it yet." It is not a matter of conviction but of a rebellious heart that manifests a love for their sin.

Christians are not to yield themselves to unrighteous living. Righteousness is not a personal conviction. The Word of God determines righteousness. "Even after an individual trusts Christ, sin is still decided by the Word of God; and he is not to sin! Sin is sin whether convicted about it or not. God's Word, Old or New Testament, is the final determinant of right and wrong regardless of a person's conviction."[13]

Profitability of the Law

God does not throw the Bible away after people become believers. Believers are not to act as if they can do anything they want because now they are free to live by their conscience. Many rebellious Christians misapply Romans 7:6, which says, "But now we have been released from the Law, having died to that by which we were bound, so that we serve in newness of the Spirit and not in oldness of the letter." The law that sentenced them to perdition no longer binds believers. Instead, they are free from the bondage of the law that condemned

---

12 Those who call other Christians legalistic as a defense for their unrighteous behavior have wrongly defined the word. As explained earlier in this chapter, legalism is attempting salvation using human works.

13 Mike Allison, Legalism—A Smokescreen. *Good News Broadcaster*, June 1985, 52.

them to death because of their sin. They now serve God with a desire to obey and please Him. The Old Testament law still has a role in that it shows men that sin after salvation is still wrong.

Five times in Matthew 5, Jesus made a statement like "You have heard that it was said" followed by "but I say to you."[14] Each time, He mentioned an Old Testament principle and taught them it was important to obey that principle. "Jesus taught that obedience goes farther than just the outward appearance. Obedience should come from a right heart attitude."[15] Jesus was teaching them that following the letter of the law was not enough. The Jews had tried that and failed miserably. Christians can obey outwardly but still be corrupt with inward sin. True inward obedience produces genuine outward obedience.

Also in Matthew 5, Jesus mentioned two of the Ten Commandments to show that Christian responsibility is much greater than obedience to the letter of the law. He used the same arguments concerning marriage and divorce, swearing an oath, personal vengeance, and loving others. In each case, there was no provision to set aside the law due to a personal conviction. Instead, under the gospel of grace, an even greater obedience is expected. Now that Jesus fulfilled the Law, the spirit of the Law goes farther in holiness than the letter of the Law.

Throughout the New Testament, there are statements that proclaim the authority of the Old Testament as a standard of holiness. One of the most clear is 2 Timothy 3:16–17. "All Scripture is inspired by God and profitable for teaching, for reproof, for correction, for training in righteousness; so that the man of God may be adequate, equipped for every good work."

Paul shows that *all* Scripture comes from God. When Paul wrote this, he was speaking of the Old Testament. In this era, it is every word of every book in both Testaments. And every word of every book in both Testaments is profitable for doctrine.

---

14 Matthew 5:21, 27, 33, 38, and 43.
15 Allison, 52-53.

Peter quotes Leviticus 11:33 in 1 Peter 1:14–16. "As obedient children, do not be conformed to the former lusts *which were yours* in your ignorance, but like the Holy One who called you, be holy yourselves also in all your behavior; because it is written, You shall be holy, for I am holy." Even though Peter includes a passage from Leviticus in his epistle, some Christians still protest, claiming they are not under the Old Testament anymore. Now they have liberty in Christ. That is a craven misuse of liberty. In fact, it is denying the authority of Scripture given by God to guide believers toward holy living. The Old Testament law is not just a guideline, it is the Word of God, and it is profitable "for training in righteousness."

Certainly keeping the Law cannot gain us salvation, but salvation causes us to keep the law, not by obligation or as a way to earn merit, but as the natural outpouring of the new life within us.

This is not legalism. It is not blind adherence to conduct based upon a set of external rules. Some believers quote only verses that have to do with liberty and freedom in Christ because they are afraid of having the label of a legalist. We ought to rejoice at having liberty in Christ, but we must never forget that it is liberty from sin, not freedom to sin. Lying, stealing, adultery, and blasphemy are acts that violate God's law. True faith changes a man's heart and subsequently his behavior. After salvation, men have deliverance from sin and wicked living. Now they can live a life that honors God in the most practical ways. Professing faith without true faith is what Paul taught Titus: "They profess to know God, but by *their* deeds they deny *Him*, being detestable and disobedient and worthless for any good deed" (Titus 1:16).

"What then? Shall we sin because we are not under law but under grace? May it never be" (Rom. 6:15)! We cannot expect that grace will permit an easier treatment of men or a relaxation of the duties to God or from the obligation to do right and obey the Scriptures. Forgiveness of sin leading to salvation is a structure upon which men must build a new and better life. God expects more of men who claim Christ as

Savior. God expects more of a Christian than He does from the Jews who live by the law.

When Scripture says, "we are not under the law, but under grace," it is referring to the means of justification. "By the works of the Law no flesh will be justified in His sight; for through the Law *comes* the knowledge of sin" (Rom. 3:20). We are saved by grace through faith. "Keeping the law is not the way to salvation."[16] Our salvation is by faith. Faith comes from God. He strengthens faith by putting His laws in our hearts. "This is the covenant that I will make with them after those days, says the Lord: I will put My laws upon their heart, and on their mind I will write them" (Heb. 10:16). The writer of Hebrews, quoting Jeremiah, is rehearsing the covenant promise that God has made to His people. Jeremiah spoke to the Jews, but in the new covenant, the promise is to all men who believe. God promised to create a regenerate people with the law of God in their minds and hearts. He is speaking of men who delight in the law. With the heart renewed, the mind welcomes divine law. When Christ gives a command, He imparts the power for us to fulfill it.

CANNOT SEPARATE LAW FROM GRACE

A relationship exists between Law and Gospel and grace that is central to understanding the Bible. Thomas Johnson writes, "The biblical interpreter has not properly examined the Scriptures if this relation between Law and Gospel has not been perceived."[17]

"The whole purpose of grace, in a sense, is just to enable us to keep the law."[18] God commands His people to be holy. Living a holy life means living righteously. Righteous living is keeping the law. To some that may sound extreme, a violation of conventional theology, but every Christian will agree that it is right to obey the Ten Commandments,

16 Harold Vaughn, An Unscriptural Division. *The Baptist Examiner.* June 11, 1998, 1, 8, 9.

17 Thomas K. Johnson, Law and Gospel. *Evangelical Review of Theology,* vol. 36, no. 2, April 2012, 158.

18 D. Martyn Lloyd-Jones, *Studies in the Sermon on the Mount.* (Grand Rapids, MI: William B. Eerdmans Publishing Company, 1976), 172.

which are the foundation of the law. Everything else that is in the law simply expands upon the Ten Commandments. "He who has My commandments and keeps them is the one who loves Me; and he who loves Me will be loved by My Father, and I will love him and will disclose Myself to him" (John 14:21). Jesus is speaking of God, His Father and the Old Testament commandments, which were still in effect during His earthly ministry. These words of our Savior are a clear injunction for believers to obey the commandments of the law. The work of Christ on Calvary, the coming of the Holy Spirit at Pentecost, or living in the age of grace has not nullified obedience to the law. They are still in effect for all. The entire idea of Christ's dying a substitutionary death so clearly written in Isaiah 53 depends upon the law being valid. Sinners must die for their sins as revealed in the law. But God is merciful and supplied a substitute to die for sinful men. Christ's death was punishment for all the sins of all mankind revealed in the law in accordance with the law. That is grace!

In Leviticus 22:31 God gives a clear command. "So you shall keep My commandments, and do them; I am the Lord." The phrase *I am the Lord* establishes God's authority and His right to require obedience to His commandments written in the law. Jesus took care to teach, "I and the Father are one" (John 10:30). Thus, His statement, "If you love Me, you will keep My commandments" (John 14:15) carries with it all the authority of God the Father. Jesus explained, "If you keep My commandments, you will abide in My love; just as I have kept My Father's commandments and abide in His love" (John 15:10). The command in Leviticus 22:31 and Jesus' words in John 14:15 are from the same Triune God. Both are valid no matter which Testament contains them.

The benefits of obedience to God's commandments are eternal: "Oh that they had such a heart in them, that they would fear Me and keep all My commandments always, that it may be well with them and with their sons forever" (Deut. 5:29)! The benefits of obedience to the commandments of God are in both Testaments. "He who has My commandments and keeps them is the one who loves Me; and he who loves Me will be loved by My Father, and I will love him and will disclose Myself to him" (John 14:21). In his first epistle, John points out how keeping the commandments is evidence of living a Christian life. "By this we know that we love the children of God, when we love God and observe His commandments. For this is the love of God, that we keep His commandments; and His commandments are not burdensome" (1 John 5:2–3). The love expected in the Christian life is well known, even among unbelievers. John is writing of true love irrevocably connected to obedience to God's Old Testament commandments through obedience to the Lord Jesus Christ.

"Christ redeemed us from the curse of the Law" (Gal. 3:13). The Law will never go away, but Calvary made it palatable. "Who also made us adequate *as* servants of a new covenant, not of the letter but of the Spirit; for the letter kills, but the Spirit gives life" (2 Cor. 3:6). The literal rites, ceremonies, and sacrifices are fulfilled. The indwelling Holy Spirit leads to a full disclosure of the true intent and meaning of the law. "But now we have been released from the Law, having died to that by which we were bound, so that we serve in newness of the Spirit and not in oldness of the letter" (Rom. 7:6). The "oldness of the letter" is the "old way of literal, mechanical obedience to the divine law, as a set of external rules of conduct, and without any reference to the state of our hearts."[19]

The law required obedience without giving power to obey. That condemns every transgression and every unholy thought without providing for pardon of sin. Christians, unlike the Old Testament saints, are under the merciful Gospel of grace. Just like the Law, the Gospel requires the strictest conformity to the will of God. It differs from the Law in that it supplies Holy Spirit power to obey. Shall we abuse our high and holy calling in Christ because we are not under that law, but are under the Gospel? Shall we sin because grace abounds? Shall we do evil that good may come of it? In the words of Paul: "May it never be!"

---

19 Jamieson, 1156.

CHAPTER 11

BIBLICIST VIEW REVISITED

FROM THE BIBLICAL EVIDENCE, THE Mosaic Law is valid in the Church Age. Not as a means of salvation, but as a set of principles to show the mind of God and guide believers in right living. Calvin declared, "It must ever remain an indubitable truth, that the Law has lost none of its authority, but must always receive from us the same respect and obedience."[1] Calvin's words are still correct some 500 years after he wrote them.

This book speaks of several truths:

- God is the author of both the Old Testament and the New Testament.

- The Law gave men an awareness of their transgressions against a holy God.

- No man could perfectly obey the Law.

- The Law pointed to a Prophet who would speak the Word of God.

- The Lord Jesus Christ is the culmination of all the shadows, ceremonies, and prophecies contained in the Old Testament.

- The Lord Jesus Christ lived the Law perfectly.

- The death and resurrection of the Lord Jesus Christ fulfilled the Law.

- Christ, the apostles, and the churches in Acts used the Old Testament.

---

1 John Calvin, Institutes, 2.7.15.

- Fulfilling the Law did not eliminate any of the Law.

- Fulfilling the Law removes men from rigid adherence to a set of commands and involves the attitude of the heart.

- Fulfilling the Law gave the commands of the Law a new richer, greater depth tempered by grace.

- The indwelling Holy Spirit gives believers the desire and ability to obey God's law.

Moses reminds the people that God commands obedience "for our good." "So the LORD commanded us to observe all these statutes, to fear the LORD our God for our good always and for our survival, as *it is* today. It will be righteousness for us if we are careful to observe all this commandment before the LORD our God, just as He commanded us" (Deut. 6:24–25). In giving the law, there is a great motive on the part of God. The Lord's nature is "for our good" always. Obeying the commandments of the Lord is the key to usefulness and happiness in the Christian life. Jesus said, "For My yoke is easy, and My burden is light" (Matt. 11:30). John added, "For this is the love of God, that we keep His commandments: and His commandments are not burdensome" (1 John 5:3). Our Lord said: "If you love Me, you will keep My commandments" (John 14:15).

When we obey God, he imputes unto us righteousness. Moses from the very beginning made the whole "righteousness of the Law: to depend entirely on a right state of the heart, in one work, on faith."[2] God would view as righteous those who obey His commands. In a strictly legal sense, that required absolute, perfect obedience to the law. Any offense, and there are many since living in perfect obedience to the law is impossible, is sufficient to condemn. All is not lost, for "Christ redeemed us from the curse of the Law, having become a curse for us" (Gal. 3:13). Our hope is in Christ who "is the end of the law for

2 Albert Barnes, *Notes on the Old Testament, Explanatory and Practical,* vol. Exodus – Ruth. ed. Robert Frew, 16th printing. (Grand Rapids, MI: Baker Book House, 1949, reprint 1978), 284.

righteousness to everyone who believes" (Rom. 10:4). In Him, we are justified because He fulfilled the Law and abolished its penalty. Christ covered our sins and justified believers.

The gospel has a foundation built on the law. All its sacrifices, types, ceremonies, and prophecies point to the gospel. The gospel acknowledges there is a law and fulfills it. The gospel upholds the law in that there are legal penalties for sin. The gospel upholds the law because of what the law says about the lives of God's people. "The detailed stipulations of the Mosaic Law often reveal principles that are part of God's Word to His people in both covenants, and believers continue to profit from what the law teaches in this respect."[3] Calvin agrees:

> "Some unskillful persons, from not attending to this, boldly discard the whole Law of Moses, and do away with both its tables, imagining it unchristian to adhere to a doctrine which contains the ministration of death. Far from our thoughts be this profane notion. Moses has admirably shown that the Law, which can produce nothing but death in sinners, ought to have a better and more excellent effect upon the righteous. When about to die, he thus addressed the people, 'Take to your heart all the words with which I am warning you today, which you shall command your sons to observe carefully, *even* all the words of this law. For it is not an idle word for you; indeed it is your life. And by this word you will prolong your days in the land, which you are about to cross the Jordan to possess'" (Deut. 32:46–47).[4]

The more Christians understand justification, the more they will value the law. The law is right in condemning men as sinners. Believers should value how Jesus Christ took their punishment under the law. If God's people love Him, they will also love and obey the law, His law.

---

3 Douglas J. Moo, *The Law of Christ as the Fulfillment of the Law of Moses: A Modified Lutheran View.* in Gundry, Stanley N. ed. *Five Views of Law and the Gospel,* (Grand Rapids: Zondervan, 1996), 376.
4 John Calvin, Institutes, 2.7.13.

THREE USES OF THE LAW[5]

In the Church Age, the law is useful in all aspects of human living, for the lost to draw them to God and for the Christian in their walk with God.

- It is a mirror into which a person looks to know his sin and misery.

- The law serves as a check on the unregenerate. It exerts a restraining influence to prevent men from giving full rein to the corruption that naturally oozes from a deceitful heart. "They show the work of the Law written in their hearts, their conscience bearing witness and their thoughts alternately accusing or else defending them" (Rom. 2:15).

- The law is a rule of divine worship and the believer's life of gratitude before God. For the Christian, the law serves as a rule that instructs him, as teacher and guide, in the will of God.

WHY THE BIBLICIST VIEW?

Myron Houghton writes, "As a theological method, an authentic evangelical theology will examine and evaluate every doctrine in light of the gospel. This has yet to be done!"[6] This book is not a theological system, but using the biblicist view, it does examine the Law in the light of the gospel.

The biblicist view is absolutely essential. Many good men differ on fine points of theology. Some minor issues may not matter, and

---

5 R. Brainsma, The Third Use of the Law. *Standard Bearer*. October 15, 2002, 38. Brainsma borrows his theme, without attribution, from Calvin's Institutes, 2.7.7, 2.7.10, and 2.7.12. Calvin explains that men often go astray like wandering sheep, but God draws them back to Him in sorrow and repentance, using the power of His Law. He describes the Law as a lamp shining in the darkness to illumine our pathway. He calls the Law a guide to eternity and the perfect rule for a thankful life in obedience and prayer.

6 Houghton makes this declaration in the first chapter. He promptly undermines this sensible statement with 194 pages defending a theological method designed by men. Myron Houghton, *Law and Grace*. (Schaumburg, IL: Regular Baptist Books, 2011), 20.

being content to wait until reaching heaven to learn the truth is perfectly acceptable.

Major issues are different. Disagreement and contention among Christians plays right into the hand of unbelievers who see the Bible as having no meaning. Their oft-repeated excuse for rejecting Christ, "You can interpret the Bible any way you want." becomes the theologian's sin.

Think about the confusion new believers must have when they hear arguments over doctrine. How many uneducated Christians leave the church because of disagreements among scholars and theologians over what ought to be settled doctrine? Tragically, many scholars and theologians give the average church member the impression of always learning and yet "never able to come to the knowledge of the truth" (2 Tim. 3:7).

Theological systems are human efforts. Scholars determine what they believe, but it may not come from Bible study. Many good men accept what they learned in their church or denomination without question. They may build their ministry on the position of the college they attended or what they learned from a favorite professor. To stay consistent with their beliefs, they often force themselves to ignore passages of Scripture that conflict with their theological system.

The practice of finding a proof text is common where they select verses, seemingly at random and jerked out of context, from anywhere in the Bible to support their position. They have their position, so they find a verse to back it up. Bruce Ware, in a volume on differing views of baptism, has some telling words. Fill in the blank with any theological topic where good men differ. He wrote, "Hence to apply this teaching to _____ goes beyond the text of Scripture and does so strictly for prior theological interests that are at best brought to the text, not drawn out of the text."[7]

---

7 Bruce Ware, Ba*ptism: Three Views.* David F. Wright, ed. (Downers Grove, IL: IVP Academic, 2009), 118.

There is one more, very important thing to emphasize before ending this book. Think of all the areas of difference in Christendom besides the issue of Law and Gospel: modes of baptism, infant baptism versus believers baptism, pre-trib, mid-trib, or post-trib, covenant versus dispensationalism, degrees of separation, music, and so on.

Nearly everyone who reads the previous paragraph will pick out the doctrinal position they believe and accept it as correct theology. Don't be too sure, when Christians have different positions on a biblical issue, one of them is wrong. If there are three positions, then at least two of them are wrong. Those last two sentences should frighten and humble every Christian. Without reference to any denominational bias or theological system, apply the biblicist view to every belief. Only then can the Christian have confidence that what they believe is right.

Preachers constantly uphold the Bereans to their congregations for searching the Scriptures: "for they received the word with great eagerness, examining the Scriptures daily *to see* whether these things were so" (Acts 17:11). Pastors properly emphasize the need for Christians to read the Bible. Rarely is the final phrase, "*to see* whether these things were so," preached with equal fervor. Yet, it is the more important phrase in order to ensure doctrinal purity and true orthodoxy.

When dealing with the Word of God, there is a great responsibility to get it right. Do not enter into theological discussions on confusing issues with total confidence in one's position. Preachers and Bible teachers must have a genuine fear of teaching an untruth. Be humble and open to learning something new from God.

THEME SCRIPTURE PASSAGE

MATTHEW 5:17–20

The New American Standard Bible is the translation used for this book. In some instances, because of familiar words and phrasing, quotes come from the King James Version. On several occasions, for the sake of clarity or for a better illustration to show context, references and quotes may come from several other translations.

The intent of this book rests on the theme passage of Matthew 5:17–20. That passage from each translation used is shown here.

New American Standard Bible

> [17]Do not think that I came to abolish the Law or the Prophets; I did not come to abolish but to fulfill.

> [18]For truly I say to you, until heaven and earth pass away, not the smallest letter or stroke shall pass from the Law until all is accomplished.

> [19]Whoever then annuls one of the least of these commandments, and teaches others *to do* the same, shall be called least in the kingdom of heaven; but whoever keeps and teaches *them*, he shall be called great in the kingdom of heaven.

²⁰For I say to you that unless your righteousness surpasses *that* of the scribes and Pharisees, you will not enter the kingdom of heaven.

King James Version

¹⁷Think not that I am come to destroy the law, or the prophets: I am not come to destroy, but to fulfill.

¹⁸For verily I say unto you, Till heaven and earth pass, one jot or one tittle shall in no wise pass from the law, till all be fulfilled.

¹⁹Whosoever therefore shall break one of these least commandments, and shall teach men so, he shall be called the least in the kingdom of heaven: but whosoever shall do and teach them, the same shall be called great in the kingdom of heaven.

²⁰For I say unto you, that except your righteousness shall exceed the righteousness of the scribes and Pharisees, ye shall in no case enter into the kingdom of heaven.

English Standard Version

¹⁷Do not think that I have come to abolish the Law or the Prophets; I have not come to abolish them but to fulfill them.

¹⁸ For truly, I say to you, until heaven and earth pass away, not an iota, not a dot, will pass from the Law until all is accomplished.

¹⁹ Therefore whoever relaxes one of the least of these commandments and teaches others to do the same will be called

least in the kingdom of heaven, but whoever does them and teaches them will be called great in the kingdom of heaven.

20 For I tell you, unless your righteousness exceeds that of the scribes and Pharisees, you will never enter the kingdom of heaven.

Amplified Bible

17 Do not think that I have come to do away with *or* undo the Law or the Prophets; I have come not to do away with *or* undo but to complete *and* fulfill them.

18 For truly I tell you, until the sky and earth pass away *and* perish, not one smallest letter nor one little hook [identifying certain Hebrew letters] will pass from the Law until all things [it foreshadows] are accomplished.

19 Whoever then breaks *or* does away with *or* relaxes one of the least [important] of these commandments and teaches men so shall be called least [important] in the kingdom of heaven, but he who practices them and teaches others to do so shall be called great in the kingdom of heaven.

20 For I tell you, unless your righteousness (your uprightness and your right standing with God) is more than that of the scribes and Pharisees, you will never enter the kingdom of heaven.

Darby Translation

17 Think not that I am come to make void the law or the prophets; I am not come to make void, but to fulfil.

[18] For verily I say unto you, Until the heaven and the earth pass away, one iota or one tittle shall in no wise pass from the law till all come to pass.

[19] Whosoever then shall do away with one of these least commandments, and shall teach men so, shall be called least in the kingdom of the heavens; but whosoever shall practice and teach [them], *he* shall be called great in the kingdom of the heavens.

[20] For I say unto you, that unless your righteousness surpass [that] of the scribes and Pharisees, ye shall in no wise enter into the kingdom of the heavens.

TWO DIFFICULT PASSAGES

Any scholarly discussion of the role of the law in the Church Age eventually turns to Leviticus 18:5 and its several quotes in the New Testament. Scholars spill much ink arguing what Moses really meant. Much the same thing occurs with Romans 10:4.

Though it is not the intent of this book to air the dissenting views on the efficacy of the law in this age, the frequency in which these two verses appear in discussions on this issue makes it necessary to address this, not by refuting their arguments, but by exegesis of the passages.

LEVITICUS 18:5

"So you shall keep My statutes and My judgments, by which a man may live if he does them; I am the Lord."

Moses used this same statement in Deuteronomy 27:26. The Levites quoted it in Nehemiah 9:29 in a prayer service where they summarized Israel's history and their frequent disobedience to God and His law. Ezekiel quoted it three times in his prophecy (Ezek. 20:11, 13, 21) where he reminded them of the failures of their past that brought them into captivity. In the New Testament, Paul quoted this verse in Romans 10:5 and Galatians 3:10.

Leviticus 18:5 in the Complete Jewish Bible reads, "You are to observe my laws and rulings; if a person does them, he will have life through them; I am ADONAI."[1] The idea is this: I am Jehovah who is

1 Comments on Leviticus 18:5 from the Complete Jewish Bible (CJB), Copyright

holy, righteous, and just with all authority to issue commands for my Creation to follow. I am Jehovah who can legitimately place on man moral and spiritual demands with an obligation to obey. The one who observes and obeys shall live happily in the land. The context of the passage indicates the land is Canaan, the Promised Land.

The sexual perversions listed in Leviticus 18, along with idolatry and other vile sins mentioned elsewhere in Leviticus, were a natural part of the culture in both Egypt and Canaan. God wants His people to avoid such practices. "They are to do God's judgments, and to keep his ordinances, that they may live in the land. The idea here is to avoid the doings of the land of Egypt and in the land of Canaan, the worshipping of demons and beasts mentioned in preceding chapters, and the abominations mentioned in this chapter."[2]

God promised a special blessing to Israel provided they obeyed the divine law. "This promise was remarkably verified in several eras of their history, when pure and undefiled religion prevailed among them, in the public prosperity and domestic happiness enjoyed by them as a people."[3] Obedience to the divine law always ensures temporal advantages in this life. No doubt, that was the meaning of the words, "by which a man may live if he does them." This is a powerful argument why they should follow God's commands, rather than the customs of men, because their life and happiness in the land depend upon it.

Moses adds to the command in Deuteronomy 27:26, "Cursed is he who does not confirm the words of this law by doing them. And all the people shall say, Amen." Men who plan to live according to the law are under the curse of the law. If one accepts part of the law, then they must accept all of the law. Living by the law is impossible because to choose to obey one part requires obeying the entire law. "However, the

© 1998 by David H. Stern. All rights reserved.
2 Commentary on Leviticus 18:1–5. Adam Clarke, *Commentary on the Whole Bible*. (Tempe, AZ: The Crosswire Software and Bible Society, 1810/1825).
3 Commentary on Leviticus 18:5. Robert Jamieson, A. R. Fausset, David Brown, *Commentary: Practical and Explanatory on the Whole Bible*. Tempe, AZ: The Crosswire Software and Bible Society).

Law is not of faith; on the contrary, 'He who practices them shall live by them'" (Gal. 3:12). The law is a list of deeds and actions. It promises no deliverance, but requires obedience. Adherents of the law do not have to believe, only do. The law does not require faith.

Supposedly, the animal sacrifices provided a pardon for failing to keep the law perfectly. Two things are important to remember. "First, the smallest failure meant the law was broken. Second, the blood of animal sacrifices could not take away sins."[4] "By the works of the Law no flesh will be justified in His sight" (Rom. 3:20). Only the perfect blood sacrifice of the Lord Jesus Christ on Calvary can justify men.

"The real difficulty with Leviticus 18:5 is not its contextual meaning but the way the New Testament uses the verse."[5] When the rich young ruler asked Jesus who would inherit eternal life, Jesus responded by asking what was in the law. In answer to Jesus, the young man quoted Deuteronomy 6:5 and Leviticus 19:18 (Luke 10:27). Jesus said he was correct and added, "do this and you will live" in verse 28. Jesus is speaking of eternal life. In Leviticus, the word "live" means in the Promised Land. When Christ quoted Moses, He added an eternal dimension for life in the hereafter.

The rich young ruler was likely under conviction, and his question of Jesus was an attempt to justify his adherence to Pharisaic dogma. Or it may have been a vain attempt to trick Jesus into revealing He was going to subvert or replace the Law of Moses. Jesus, of course, saw the young ruler's heart was hardened to the Scriptures and he had no desire to keep God's statutes and judgments written in the Law. That is why He did not respond to his correct answer with a plan of salvation as He had done for Zacchaeus in Luke 19.

The young ruler did not want to live by the statutes and judgments of God. The immediate result of that refusal in the Old Testament

---

4 Alva J. McClain, *Law and Grace.* 1954. Reprint, (Chicago: Moody Press, 1967), 18.
5 Ken Casillas, Do this and Live: Leviticus 18:5. *Frontline Magazine Pastor's Insert,* May/June 2013, 6.

caused the Israelites to experience famine, pestilence, and invasions by conquering armies. Since they did not live by faith in God, they could not gain approval as the Old Testament saints did (Heb. 11:2, 39). The ultimate New Testament result is much worse; refusing to live by the statutes and judgments of God means eternal separation from God.

Paul refers to the curse when he quotes Deuteronomy 27:26, "For as many as are of the works of the Law are under a curse; for it is written, 'cursed is everyone who does not abide by all things written in the book of the law, to perform them'" (Gal. 3:10). The very next verse shows how this is impossible, "Now that no man is justified by the Law before God is evident for; 'the righteous man shall live by faith'" (Gal. 3:11).

James explains this in his epistle: "For whoever keeps the whole law and yet stumbles in one *point*, he has become guilty of all" (Jam. 2:10). If any man chooses to live in accordance with the Old Testament law given by Moses, then he must fully obey every part of that law. Whoever tries to keep the whole law, except for even one small point, is guilty of breaking the whole law. He is just as liable to condemnation as if he had broken every bit of the law. Thus, everyone has broken the law because no man is capable of justification by living up to the spiritual meaning and intent of the law. Our justification is in Christ by faith.

Paul agrees with James when writing that the man who tries to live by the law must obey all of the law (Gal. 5:3). In Galatians 3:10, Paul explained how those who follow the law are under the curse of the law. He is not speaking to Jews but to born-again Galatians who began to follow the rites of circumcision after the Judaizers persuaded them it was necessary. By citing Moses, he reminds them a curse accompanied those who did not obey all the law (Deut. 27:26). Like James, he reminds them of the obligation of the law, which requires obedience to every part of the law. Successful obedience is complete obedience without any exceptions.

In Romans 10:5 Paul, quoting Leviticus 18:5, explains how men achieve eternal life under the law: "For Moses writes that the man who practices the righteousness which is based on law shall live by that righteousness."

The righteousness of the law is the righteousness that men can obtain by fully obeying the law. The man who does all the things the law requires shall live by them and thus be saved by his works. Of course, that is impossible for any man. Nevertheless, if it were possible, it is a way of justification and life—by the righteousness, which is of the law.

ROMANS 10:4

"For Christ is the end of the law for righteousness to everyone who believes."

Many detractors of the law having any efficacy in the Church Age cite Romans 10:4 as evidence that the law is invalid in the Church Age. Some go so far as to use this verse to substantiate a claim that Romans 10:4 proves Matthew 5:17 ends the efficacy of the law for Christians.[6]

The context begins in the preceding chapter with Romans 9:30–33. There, Paul is comparing Gentiles saved by faith to Israelites who followed a path of religion under the law that could not lead to salvation. Their problem according to 9:32 was they pursued righteousness by works instead of by faith. The law became a stumbling stone to them. Israel was not in search of righteousness because they were certain they already had righteousness. They justified their position because they were God's chosen people and had the Law of Moses.

Unfortunately, they could not achieve righteousness through the law. Their legal religion turned out to be a failure.

Beginning in chapter 10, Paul, addressing the Roman Christians, writes of his burden for the salvation of the Jews. He acknowledges their zeal for God but points out that insufficient knowledge led them astray. In 10:3, Paul explains they have incomplete knowledge and, sadly, prefer to keep it that way. In a stinging indictment, he writes they wanted their own righteousness based upon a religion of their own

6 Douglas J. Moo, *The Law of Christ as the Fulfillment of the Law of Moses: A Modified Lutheran View* in Gundry, Stanley N. ed. *Five Views of Law and the Gospel*, (Grand Rapids: Zondervan, 1996), 359.

making that glorified them only. As part of their efforts, they refused to subject themselves to the Messiah, "to the righteousness of God."

Finally, in Romans 10:4, Paul writes that now that Christ has brought true righteousness, "law as a means of attaining righteousness has ceased."[7] Legal religion and the observance of statutes is a thing of the past, even when God Himself issued them. In this age, righteousness comes from faith in the Lord Jesus Christ. The Gospel did not terminate the Law in the sense it is finished or abolished. Only having to use the Law as a method of attaining righteousness is finished and abolished.

The Greek word translated *end* in Romans 10:4 is *telos*, which means the object, scope, or final cause; the end proposed and intended. The NASB has a footnote that suggests using the word *goal* as a rendering for *end*. Christ is the goal of the Law, not its termination. The final object, indeed the very design of the Law, its goal, is to make men righteous by bringing them to believe in Christ for justification and salvation. "The law cannot be properly understood unless it moves toward the grand goal of pointing the believer toward the Messiah, Christ."[8] That is Christ, the fulfilling of the Law.

The final word of righteousness is Jesus because he is "the way" (John 14:6). This is the culmination of the plan of God for men. Christ fulfilled the Law. Christ fulfilled all Scripture. No one can use the Law to accuse anyone because Christ fulfilled the Law forever, and salvation by grace is available.

Using Romans 10:4 as some scholars do, as a proof text declaring that Matthew 5:17 ends the efficacy of the law for Christians, fails to consider the context and is not a valid argument.

---

7 Much of the material in this explanation of Romans 10:4 comes from Kenneth S. Wuest. *Romans* in *Wuest's Word Studies from the Greek New Testament for the English Reader, Vol. 1.* (Grand Rapids, MI: William B. Eerdmans Publishing Company, 1953, reprint 1978), 169-173.

8 Walter C. Kaiser, Jr., *The Law as God's Gracious Guidance for the Promotion of Holiness* in Gundry, Stanley N. ed. *Five Views of Law and the Gospel*, (Grand Rapids: Zondervan, 1996), 188.

OTHER LAWS

Numerous places in the Bible mention "other laws." Generally, when reading one of these verses, the context makes the intent of the biblical writer clear and obvious. On other occasions, these laws have become a source of confusion to believers.

The phrase *law of* occurs seventy-six times in the King James Version of the Old Testament.[1] Forty-seven times, it clearly indicates the Mosaic Law. Four times *law of* refers to a relative such as father-in-law. Four times *law of* refers to the laws of foreign nations. Regulations concerning specific duties under various parts of ceremonial aspects of the Mosaic Law comprise another fifteen instances. One instance refers to the laws of the nation. Twice it means obedience to parents. Three times *law of* means teaching or instruction.

Most of the confusion appears to come from the New Testament. Some scholars have taken these laws of and manufactured a new law that supersedes the Mosaic Law. Law of occurs twenty-eight times in the New Testament, and twelve clearly refer to the Mosaic Law. It is variously expressed as law of Moses, law of God, law of the fathers, law of the Jews, and law of the Lord. Explanations for the rest follow.

---

1 The King James Version was used for the count because it is most well known. In the past 400 years most commentaries and other Bible literature used the KJV. The count is based upon the phrase "law of . . . " A random sampling of other English translations reveals only minor differences. One of the most common is the substitution of "principle" instead of law.

LAW OF FAITH

> "Where then is boasting? It is excluded. By what kind of law?
> Of works? No, but by a law of faith" (Rom. 3:27).

Every man is a sinner who is unable to justify himself by the law, so he has no right to boast of anything. Boasting of any glory for himself is pointless. The first word translated law has the idea of an arrangement, a rule, or principle. Paul asks two questions. What principle excludes boasting? Are there are any works of man that would permit boasting? Paul answers his own question—no, salvation is by the principle of justification by faith.

Paul was writing to Jews who tended to glory in their religion. Here he explains to converted Jews they have no reason to boast in their Jewish heritage. "The principle of the law of faith, which has been shown to be the only one available of the justification of either Jew or Gentile, in itself, excludes boasting."[2] So with the phrase "by a law of faith," Paul is teaching humility and that the principle involved in the gift of salvation by faith excludes any boasting.

LAW OF HER HUSBAND

> "For the married woman is bound by law to her husband
> while he is living; but if her husband dies, she is released
> from the law concerning the husband" (Rom. 7:2).

This verse cannot stand alone. Always consider it in context with verse one, which explains the general principle that a man is bound to whatever law he lives under while alive. Paul is showing that marriage is permanent while either spouse is alive. It is a simple principle. Death frees a man from the law of his country. His death also frees his wife to remarry. The death of a spouse releases the survivor from the marriage.

---

2 J. Barmby, Romans in *The Pulpit Commentary*, ed. H.D.M. Spence & Joseph Exell. (New York: Funk & Wagnalls, 1913), 85.

LAW OF GOD

Law of God appears three times. Two are in the same passage where Paul explains the war between the believer's old sin nature and his new nature in Christ.

> "For I delight in the law of God after the inward man" (Rom. 7:22).

> "I thank God through Jesus Christ our Lord. So then with the mind I myself serve the law of God; but with the flesh the law of sin" (Rom. 7:25).

The phrase *law of God* does point to the Mosaic Law, but it is much more. "The word *law* in both verses is used expansively, to denote all the communications which God had made to control man."[3]

Paul declares that obedience to God's holy law is of vital importance to him. The "law of God" is the Mosaic Law and any other directive from God. It includes every message from God to man, the leading of the Holy Spirit in the heart of the believer, as well as the Pentateuch, sound gospel preaching, or simply from reading anything in the Bible. Clearly, Paul is pleased with all that God has chosen to communicate.

> "Because the carnal mind is enmity against God: for it is not subject to the law of God, neither indeed can be" (Rom. 8:7).

In this third law of God verse, the meaning is the same, but there is a different emphasis. Believers who choose to pursue carnality are living in a manner that is opposed to the character and will of God. The carnal mind enjoys sin "and lives in opposition to the pure and holy law of God."[4] The carnal believer has become an enemy of God.

3 Albert Barnes, *Notes on the New Testament, Explanatory and Practical*, vol. Matthew and Mark. ed. Robert Frew, 16th printing. (Grand Rapids, MI: Baker Book House, 1949, reprint 1978), 173.
4 Comments of Romans 8:7. Adam Clarke, *Commentary on the Whole Bible*. Tempe, AZ: The Crosswire Software and Bible Society, 1810/1825.

192 A BIBLICIST VIEW OF LAW AND GOSPEL

The carnal Christian refuses obedience for he is living in sin, acting in opposition to the standard of God. Carnal living is incompatible to the law of God. The carnal mind refuses to obey any of the communication from God. "In such a state of mind there neither is nor can be the least subjection to the law of God."[5]

LAW OF SIN

This phrase, *law of sin*, occurs twice in the passage where Paul describes the internal conflict in believers who want to do right but are hindered by their inborn sin nature. The verses are as follows:

> "But I see another law in my members, warring against the law of my mind, and bringing me into captivity to the law of sin which is in my members" (Rom. 7:23).

> "I thank God through Jesus Christ our Lord. So then with the mind I myself serve the law of God; but with the flesh the law of sin" (Rom. 7:25).

The law of sin is a contrast with the "law of my mind" also in this verse 23. In speaking of the law of sin, Paul is describing the power and authority of sin and death. It is the natural inclination of men to do evil in spite of all that grace has done. No Christian, no matter how long they have known the Lord or how strong their desire to please Him, is what they ought to be. Paul is describing the conflict in all believers. When drawn under the power of a sinful nature, even men with the best of intentions to serve God are easily overcome by sin. The law of sin is the overwhelming propensity, residing naturally in all men, to do wrong and violate God's perfect standard.

5 Robert Jamieson, A. R. Fausset, David Brown, *Commentary: Practical and Explan-atory on the Whole Bible,* new and rev. ed. (Grand Rapids, Michigan: Zondervan, 1961), 1160.

LAW OF MY MIND

"But I see another law in my members, warring against the
law of my mind, and bringing me into captivity to the law
of sin which is in my members" (Rom. 7:23).

The regenerate man is not one man but two. He feels within himself a power that tends toward holiness and God, while at the same
time he is still a child of Adam's flesh. "For the flesh sets its desire
against the Spirit, and the Spirit against the flesh; for these are in opposition to one another, so that you may not do the things that you
please" (Gal. 5:17). Quite naturally, this becomes a source of distress
and struggle wholly unknown to lost men. The Holy Spirit works in
the believer to direct him into a spiritual development in accordance
with the plan and will of God.

The *law of my mind* means "the normal constitution of my higher
and better self, whereby it cannot but assent to the law of God." It
denotes the desires and purpose of a renewed heart consisting of the
desires of the heart as inspired by the indwelling Spirit.

LAW OF THE SPIRIT OF LIFE IN CHRIST & LAW OF
SIN AND DEATH

"For the law of the Spirit of life in Christ Jesus hath made me
free from the law of sin and death" (Rom. 8:2).

Chapter 7 speaks of condemnation. Chapter 8:1 reveals something
better: "Therefore there is now no condemnation for those who are
in Christ Jesus."

"The law of sin and death" is the condemning power of the Mosaic
Law, which brings guilt to the conscience because of sin and binds
men to condemnation and death.

"The law of the Spirit of life in Christ Jesus" is a new principle of
action, which the Spirit of Christ opened within us. This new law sets

men free from condemnation. This new law sets men free from the enslaving power of sin. It sets men free from the corruption of the heart and the reigning power of the law of sin and death residing in all lost men from birth.

This verse is a microcosm of the Bible. The law reveals sin and condemns unbelievers to perdition. The gospel sets men free, justifying them and purifying them of their guilt. "The law of the Spirit of life" is a new direction of the soul that occurs when the Holy Ghost indwells a new believer through faith in Christ.

LAW OF RIGHTEOUSNESS

"But Israel, which followed after the law of righteousness, hath not attained to the law of righteousness" (Rom. 9:31).

The law of righteousness denotes failure that comes from legalism. The Jews were looking for a law they could obey in order to receive justification and eternal life. They placed their trust in the Law of Moses.

Israel observed their religion pursuing a law that would justify. They sincerely and with legalistic perfection aimed at acceptance with God; nevertheless, they missed it. They trusted in their privileged position as the chosen people of God, but without faith. They were diligent in observing rules, which they thought would secure for them the blessings of God. Sadly, they did not live in obedience with true faith that would have secured all the blessings of God.

They missed their goal. They were pleased with their status as the people of God and happily followed all the rites and ceremonies of the Mosaic Law. They created hundreds of additional rules to show their seriousness. Even worse, they continued to embrace the types and shadows of Christ in the Old Testament after the substance of the shadows was come to earth.

They spent all their religious efforts in observing the fictitious law of righteousness but fell short of acceptance with God. They were not justified, for they had no faith.

LAW OF COMMANDMENTS

> "Having abolished in his flesh the enmity, *even* the law of *commandments* contained in ordinances; for to make in himself of twain one new man, *so* making peace" (Eph. 2:15).

The context is important to understanding "law of commandments." One of the purposes of the law was to keep the Jews a distinct and separate nation and people while pointing to the coming of the Messiah. Naturally, this led to a marked division that often led to animosity between the Jews and Gentiles. The Jews considered themselves privileged persons who had the only way to heaven. Gentiles scorned Jewish exclusivism and held their rites and customs in contempt. Yet, the ceremonies and rituals of the Law were a decree that worked against Israel. The Law was in opposition to the future of the nation in reference to salvation and eternal life.

Paul is also speaking of another division, which is a partition between God and man expressed as enmity or hostility and opposition by men toward God. Specifically, it was the sin of men against the wrath of God. Christ, by His death and resurrection, abolished the partition. That made it possible for the reconciliation of Jew and Gentile. Even more important, the two together become reconciled in Christ to God. Jews and Gentiles will become one new man.

The idea behind "making peace" is primarily between all men and God. Peace between Jews and Gentiles is secondary. He being our peace, the condemnation of the law died with Him "And their sins and their lawless deeds I will remember no more" (Heb. 10:17).

LAW OF CARNAL COMMANDMENT

> "Who is made, not after the law of a carnal commandment,
> but after the power of an endless life" (Heb. 7:16).

This passage speaks of Melchizedek "king of Salem, priest of the Most High God" (Heb. 7:1). It is a comparison of the earthly priesthood of the Levites with the eternal priesthood of Christ. The use of law here does not refer to the complete Mosaic Law, but to the statutes that establish the Levitical priesthood. The writer is explaining how Melchizedek was not as the Levitical priests were. All rules for qualification for the Levitical priesthood were physical.

Carnal denotes only outward and temporary, compared with *endless*. The writer contrasts *commandments* with *life*. "The law can give a commandment, but it cannot give life. But our High Priest's inherent 'power,' now in heaven, has in Him 'life forever' 'through the eternal Spirit'" (Heb. 7:25). It is in the power of His resurrection life, not of His earthly life, that Christ officiates as a Priest.[6]

An "endless life" refers to something other than a human life that lasts for a while and then dies. It refers to a life that is everlasting. It attests to the pureness and holiness of the Lord Jesus Christ. Compared with the permanent work of Christ on Calvary, "the law of a carnal commandment" can only provide a temporary priesthood whose work is ineffective for salvation.

LAW OF LIBERTY

Law of Liberty appears twice, both times in James' epistle.

> "But one who looks intently at the perfect law, the *law* of
> liberty, and abides by it, not having become a forgetful hearer

---

6 The content of this paragraph borrows heavily from Robert Jamieson, A. R. Fausset, David Brown, *Commentary: Practical and Explanatory on the Whole Bible*, new and rev. ed. (Grand Rapids, Michigan: Zondervan, 1961), 1415.

but an effectual doer, this man will be blessed in what he does" (James 1:25).

"So speak and so act as those who are to be judged by *the* law of liberty" (James 2:12).

The Greek word translated *liberty* is often translated *freedom* or used as the opposite of servitude or bondage. It applies to captives or slaves who received their freedom. James does not use the word to mean external freedom, where the possessor has the formal power to choose what he will do. Instead, it has the idea of deliverance from the captivity of sinful lusts, self-will, and moral corruption.

Therefore, the law of liberty is "the possession of holiness, with the will and ability to do what is right and good. Such liberty is possible only in a renewed condition of soul, and cannot exist apart from godliness."[7] In other words, "the perfect law of liberty is the Gospel, which gives true freedom to the soul, and is a perfect rule of action."[8] The law of liberty is the gospel of Christ, which gives believers a clear knowledge of God. The law of liberty makes possible forgiveness of sin, righteousness, and justification. It is a law that gives freedom from guilt and enslavement to the power and influence of sin.

The gospel is a law of liberty, giving us deliverance from the Jewish law, from sin and guilt, and from wrath and death. As a law, it is perfect; nothing can improve it. An "effectual doer" studies the gospel until it becomes a part of the believer's life. Christians should not forget it, should practice it daily in the home and in the workplace. It ought to be the guide for all social interactions and the framework of all thoughts and deeds so that obedience to the gospel is by instinct.

The gospel is about an internal, free, instinctive inclination to love God and man. Through God's mercy, the law of liberty frees men from

---

7 James Orr, in the International Standard Bible Encyclopedia. 1844-1913 ed. (Tempe, AZ: The Crosswire Software and Bible Society, 1810/1825).

8 Commentary on James 2:12. Family Bible Notes from the Nazarene Users Group. (Tempe, AZ: The Crosswire Software and Bible Society).

the curse of the law. The law of liberty, the gospel, through God's mercy frees Christians so they can be free to love God and willingly obey Him. For those who fail to practice love to all men that is expected of believers by the law of liberty, grace will condemn more severely than the Law of Moses, which brings wrath on those who break even the least part of it. This, too, is fulfillment of the law.

We are under the law to Christ. It is a law of liberty, and one that we have no reason to complain of as a yoke or burden; for the service of God, according to the gospel, is perfect freedom; it sets us at liberty from all slavish regards, to either persons or the things of this world.

All men face judgment by the law of liberty, and their eternal condition will be determined according to the gospel. When wicked men sin against the gospel by rejecting the Lord Jesus Christ, they are condemned. There will be no relief to those whom the gospel condemns. Christians justified by the gospel will not have any accusation made against them. According to their works, done in obedient living, they will receive rewards.

In the context of the book of James, the idea here is that God's people, freed from bondage by the law of liberty, will desire to serve God and do good works in His name: "For just as the body without *the* spirit is dead, so also faith without works is dead" (James 2:26). James' emphasis is to show that God will judge men by the law of liberty.

Christians are to respect and obey every commandment of God. Jeremiah spoke of a new covenant, "I will put My law within them and on their heart I will write it; and I will be their God, and they shall be My people" (Jer. 31:33). Christians, because of the indwelling Holy Spirit, know the law of liberty. They can expect God to hold them accountable to it.

LAW OF CHRIST

"Bear one another's burdens, and thereby fulfill the law of Christ" (Gal. 6:2).

The verse preceding this verse reminds believers to look out for their brothers who may, whether by accident, ignorance, or temptation, fall into sin. Paul instructs them of their duty to their weak brothers. God's people are to be ready to love them with gentleness and be ready to help them. Love for others is sure evidence of a child of God: "The one who loves his brother abides in the Light and there is no cause for stumbling in him" (1 John 2:10).

In this verse, Paul emphasizes the point by reminding Christians to "bear one another's burdens." The Greek word for *burden* used here means "heavy load." It is plural, which means that Christians ought to be ready to help fellow believers with all their burdens. The idea of a burden is a load that is just a bit more than a man can carry. The idea of the Greek word translated *bear* is to lift up, to help others carry their load. Christians ought to help each other.

Think about what a person goes through when overtaken by sin. Since all men sin, even Christians, it shouldn't be hard to empathize with the fallen brother. Christians should think about how they would want others to come to them if taken in sin. Then restore the brother in meekness because the day may come when they will need restoration themselves. "In everything, therefore, treat people the same way you want them to treat you, for this is the Law and the Prophets" (Matt. 7:12).

It is right to do this because it is the example of the love of Christ who gave everything to bear the burden of a fallen race. "He himself bore our sins in his body on the tree, that we might die to sin and live to righteousness. By his wounds you have been healed" (1 Pet. 2:24, ESV). Men ought to be ready to give of themselves in love to help others, give time, rights, resources, and privileges to help others, always ready to be an encouragement to fellow believers.

The idea of loving others is not new. It was the Second Great Commandment of the Law of Moses: "You shall love your neighbor as yourself; I am the Lord" (Lev. 19:18). The remainder of this passage in Leviticus lists a series of instructions that explain how an individual ought to behave toward those around him. The New Testament continues this principle with the idea of loving others as Christ loved us.

Jesus quotes Moses: "You shall love your neighbor as yourself" (Matt. 22:39). He declares this is one of the two great commandments. The first is love for God. The second describes the responsibilities men have toward other men. These words, quoted three more times by Jesus,[9] ensure that men know loving others is a requirement, a command for all Christians to obey. There is no better way to fulfill the Law of Christ than by providing loving aid and comfort to fellow believers.

Paul quotes Leviticus 19:18 in Galatians 5:13–14. "For you were called to freedom, brethren; only do not turn your freedom into an opportunity for the flesh, but through love serve one another. For the whole Law is fulfilled in one word, in the statement, 'You shall love your neighbor as yourself.'" The Greek here means "the whole law;" that is, the Mosaic Law. So the Greek phrase translated one word here denotes the fulfilling of "all the law." Paul instructs them to love one another.[10] Paul is writing to believers so his words reveal that loving in the manner of the Law of Christ is a necessary mark of identification. The injunction comes from the law; the love comes from Jesus Christ. Love is the law of Christ.

James quotes this passage: "If, however, you are fulfilling the royal law according to the Scripture, 'You shall love your neighbor as yourself,' you are doing well" (James 2:8). He alone uses the Greek term royal law. A royal law is the law that is king of all laws. God, the great King, is love; His law is the royal law of love, and that law, like

---

9 Our Lord also quotes these words of Moses in Matthew 19:19, Mark 12:31, and in Luke 10:27.
10 Paul also quotes this in Romans 10:9.

Himself, reigns supreme. Nevertheless, the love and the ability to love come from Jesus Christ, not the law.

The phrase *fulfill the law of Christ* means loving others the way Christ loves men. The Law of Christ is not the Ten Commandments or the Sermon on the Mount. The Law of Christ is love, loving one another as Christ loved us. The Law of Christ is the gospel message. John expounds on this in 1 John 3:11 when he says, "For this is the message which you have heard from the beginning, that we should love one another." Christians have an obligation to help others, especially the brethren. They are to look out for each other, for the sick, for those who are discouraged, and for those who have fallen into sin. Everyone can love and encourage others.

The Law of Christ is in the Lord's words in the many times He commanded men to love others. "A new commandment I give to you, that you love one another, even as I have loved you, that you also love one another" (John 13:34). Later he said, "This is My commandment, that you love one another, just as I have loved you" (John 15:12). John repeated the instruction: "This is His commandment, that we believe in the name of His Son Jesus Christ, and love one another, just as He commanded us" (1 John 3:23). Later John wrote, "And this commandment we have from Him, that the one who loves God should love his brother also" (1 John 4:21). Initially, lost people do not come to Christ by conviction or doctrine, but how Christians treat others. Lost people need to know Christians are a people of love. Doctrine and life are both important, but it is the life that means so much to others.

Love is the Fulfillment of the Law

"Love does no wrong to a neighbor; therefore love is the fulfillment of *the* law" (Rom. 13:10). The law fulfilled in the gospel is love in action. When men genuinely love God, love for men naturally follows. Christians will want to do good to others because it is the nature of love. A heart overflowing with true godly love causes men to delight in pleasing the object of their love.

Love itself is not a new thing with the gospel, but was from the time of Moses: "Now I ask you, lady, not as though *I* were writing to you a new commandment, but the one which we have had from the beginning, that we love one another (2 John 5). "The Old Testament implies that love is the fulfillment of the Law."[11] "What was absolutely new was this obligation of loving others as Christ has loved us."[12] His love for us became our example to love others. The New Testament treats this law of love, the Law of Christ, as the fulfillment of everything in the law concerning human relationships. "Owe nothing to anyone except to love one another; for he who loves his neighbor has fulfilled *the* law" (Rom. 13:8). Adam Clarke writes: "Love shed abroad in a believing heart, is the sum and substance of religion."[13]

---

11 A. Berkeley Mickelsen, *Romans in The Wycliffe Bible Commentary*, ed. Charles F. Pfeiffer and Everett F. Harrison. (Nashville: The Southwestern Co., 1962), 1221.

12 Alva McClain, *Law and Grace*. 1954. Reprint, (Chicago: Moody Press, 1967), 77.

13 Commentary on 1 Corinthians 7:19. Adam Clarke. *Commentary on the Whole Bible. Tempe, AZ: The Crosswire Software and Bible Society, 1810/1825.*

BIBLIOGRAPHY

Adeney, W. F. Matthew, vol. 1 in *The Pulpit Commentary*, ed. H.D.M. Spence & Joseph Exell. New York: Funk & Wagnalls, 1913.

Aldridge, Roy L. The Mosaic Ten Commandments Compared to their Restatements in the New Testament. *Bibliotheca Sacra*. July 1961, 251.

Alexander, W. L. and Clemance, C. Deuteronomy in *The Pulpit Commentary*, ed. H.D.M. Spence & Joseph Exell. New York: Funk & Wagnalls, 1913.

Allison, Mike. Legalism—A Smokescreen. *Good News Broadcaster*, June 1985, 51–53.

Bahnsen, Greg L. The Theonomic Reformed Approach to Law and Gospel. in Gundry, Stanley N. ed. Five Views of Law and the Gospel, Grand Rapids: Zondervan, 1996.

_____Response to *The Law of Christ as the Fulfillment of the Law of Moses: A Modified Lutheran View* by Douglas J. Moo in Gundry, Stanley N. ed. *Five Views of Law and the Gospel*, Grand Rapids: Zondervan, 1996.

Barmby, J. Romans. in *The Pulpit Commentary*, ed. H.D.M. Spence & Joseph Exell. New York: Funk & Wagnalls, 1913.

Brainsma, R. The Third Use of the Law. *Standard Bearer*. October 15, 2002, 37–39.

Barnes, Albert. *Notes on the New Testament, Explanatory and Practical,* vol. Ephesians-Colossians. ed. Robert Frew, 16th printing. Grand Rapids, MI: Baker Book House, 1949, reprint 1978.

_____*Notes on the New Testament, Explanatory and Practical,* vol. Matthew and Mark. ed. Robert Frew, 16th printing. Grand Rapids, MI: Baker Book House, 1949, reprint 1978.

_____*Notes on the New Testament, Explanatory and Practical,* Romans. vol. III. ed. Robert Frew, 16th printing. Grand Rapids, MI: Baker Book House, 1949, reprint 1978.

_____*Notes on the Old Testament, Explanatory and Practical,* Proverbs – Ezekiel. ed. F.C. Cook, 14th printing. Grand Rapids, MI: Baker Book House, 1953, reprint 1978.

Boice, James Montgomery. *The Sermon on the Mount.* Grand Rapids, MI, Baker Books, 1972.

Burroughs, Jeremiah. The Evil of Evils: The Exceeding Sinfulness of Sin. (1599–1646).

Caffin, B.C. Matthew, vol. 1 in *The Pulpit Commentary,* ed. H.D.M. Spence & Joseph Exell. New York: Funk & Wagnalls, 1913.

Cairns, Alan, ed. *Dictionary of Theological Terms.* 2nd ed. Greenville, SC: Ambassador-Emerald International, 1998.

Calvin, John. *Institutes.* Trans: Henry Beveridge. Peabody, MA: Hendrickson Publishers, 2008.

Casillas, Ken. Do this and Live: Leviticus 18:5. *Frontline Magazine Pastor's Insert,* May/June 2013, 6.

_____*The Law and the Christian.* Greenville, SC: Bob Jones University Press, 2007.

Caven, William. The Testimony of Christ to the Old Testament, in *The Fundamentals*, vol. 1 R. A. Torrey, ed. reprint 1996, Grand Rapids, MI: Baker Books, 1917.

Cheyne, T. K. Jeremiah. vol. 11 in *The Pulpit Commentary*, ed. H.D.M. Spence & Joseph Exell. New York: Funk & Wagnalls, 1913.

Clarke, Adam. *Commentary on the Whole Bible.* Tempe, AZ: The Crosswire Software and Bible Society, 1810/1825.

Comfort, Ray. The Preaching of the Law is Hell's Best Kept Secret. Herald of His Coming, Vol. 48, No. 12, December 1989, 1, 3.

Conway, S. Jeremiah. vol. 11 in *The Pulpit Commentary*, ed. H.D.M. Spence & Joseph Exell. New York: Funk & Wagnalls, 1913.

Couch, Mal, ed. *The Fundamentals for the Twenty-First Century.* Grand Rapids, MI: Kregel Publications, 2000.

Davies, J. Newton. Matthew in *The Abingdon Bible Commentary.* Frederick C. Eiselen, Edwin Lewis, and David G. Downey ed. New York, Abingdon-Cokesbury Press, 1929.

Davis, John D. *A Dictionary of the Bible.* 4th rev. ed. Grand Rapids, MI: Baker Book House, 1954.

Delitzsch, Franz. *Old Testament History of Redemption.* trans. Samuel I. Curtis. Edinburgh: T.&T. Clark; reprint 1988, Peabody, MA: Hendrickson Publishers, 1881.

Ellis, E. Earle. Colossians in *The Wycliffe Bible Commentary*, ed. Charles F. Pfeiffer and Everett F. Harrison. Nashville: The Southwestern Co., 1962.

Family Bible Notes from the Nazarene Users Group. (Tempe, AZ: The Crosswire Software and Bible Society).

Farrar, F. W. *The Epistle of Paul the Apostle to the Hebrews* in The Cambridge Bible for Schools and Colleges, ed. J.J.S. Perowne. Cambridge: University Press, 1893.

Fee, Gordon, Douglas Stuart. *How to Read the Bible for all Its Worth.* 3rd ed. Grand Rapids, MI: Zondervan, 2003.

Findlay, G. G. Colossians in *The Pulpit Commentary,* ed. H.D.M. Spence & Joseph Exell. New York: Funk & Wagnalls, 1913.

Gray, James M. *Christians Workers' Bible Commentary.* Westwood, NJ: Fleming H. Revell Company, 1953.

Graybill, John F. *Jeremiah* in *The Wycliffe Bible Commentary,* ed. Charles F. Pfeiffer and Everett F. Harrison. Nashville: The Southwestern Co., 1962.

Gundry, Stanley N. ed. *Five Views of Law and the Gospel,* Grand Rapids: Zondervan, 1996.

Harding, Michael. Preserved for Proclamation and Transformation, In *God's Word in our Hands.* James B. Williams, ed. Greenville, SC: Ambassador-Emerald International, 2003.

Henry, Matthew. *Complete Commentary on the Whole Bible.* Public Domain. This text was prepared from the Christian Classics Ethereal Library located at www.ccel.org. Tempe, AZ. The Crosswire Software and Bible Society.

Hodge, Charles. *Systematic Theology.* Vol. 3, Peabody, MA: Hendrickson Publishers: 2008.

Hornung, Paul in a sermon preached at Grace Baptist Church, Landrum, SC on 22 June 2011.

Houghton, Myron. *Law and Grace.* Schaumburg, IL: Regular Baptist Books, 2011.

Jamieson, Robert, A. R. Fausset, David Brown. *Commentary: Practical and Explanatory on the Whole Bible,* new and rev. ed. Grand Rapids, Michigan: Zondervan, 1961.

Johnson, Thomas K. Law and Gospel. E*vangelical Review of Theology,* vol. 36, no. 2, April 2012, 151.

Josephus Antiquities 4.8.3, 4.8.44

Kaiser, Jr., Walter C. *Toward Rediscovering the Old Testament.* Paperback edition, 1991. Grand Rapids, MI: Zondervan Publishing House, 1987.

_____Response to *The Inauguration of the Law of Christ with the Gospel of Christ: A Dispensational View.* by Wayne Strickland in Gundry, Stanley N. ed. *Five Views of Law and the Gospel,* Grand Rapids: Zondervan, 1996.

_____Response to *The Law is the Perfection of Righteousness in Jesus Christ: A Reformed Perspective* Willem A. VanGemeren in *Five views on Law and Gospel,* by Stanley N. Gundry. ed. Grand Rapids: Zondervan, 1996.

Kent, Homer A. Matthew in *The Wycliffe Bible Commentary,* ed. Charles F. Pfeiffer and Everett F. Harrison. Nashville: The Southwestern Co., 1962.

Kline, Meredith G. *Deuteronomy* in *The Wycliffe Bible Commentary,* ed. Charles F. Pfeiffer and Everett F. Harrison. Nashville: The Southwestern Co., 1962.

Kraeling, Emil G. *The Old Testament since the Reformation.* New York: Harper, 1955.

Lightfoot, J.B. *Colossians and Philemon.* Wheaton, IL: Crossway Books, 1997.

Lloyd-Jones, D. Martyn. *Studies in the Sermon on the Mount.* Grand Rapids, MI: William B. Eerdmans Publishing Company, 1976.

Lockman Foundation, The Bible. *The New American Standard Version*, The Foundation Press Publications, La Habra, CA, 1971.

Luther, Martin. *What Luther Says*, vol. 1, compiled by Ewald M. Plass St. Louis: Concordia, 1959.

_____*Luther's Commentary on Galatians*. Tempe, AZ: The Crosswire Software and Bible Society.

_____*Luther's Works*, ed. and trans. Jaroslav Pelikan, assoc. ed. Walter A Hansen, vol. 26: Lectures on Galatians, 1535. St. Louis: Concordia Publishing House, 1963.

Manley, G. T. "The New Bible Handbook," Chicago: The Intervarsity Christian Fellowship, 1949, 442–455, quoted in W. T. Purkiser, Demaray, C.E., Metz, Donald S., Stuneck, Maude A., *Exploring the Old Testament*, (Kansas City, MO: Beacon Hill Press of Kansas City, 1955), 48.

Martin, William C. *The Layman's Bible Encyclopedia*. Nashville: The Southwestern Co., 1964.

McAvoy, Steven L. Can Truth Be Known? In Mal Couch, ed. *The Fundamentals for the Twenty-first Century*. Grand Rapids, MI: Kregel Publications, 2000.

McClain, Alva J. *Law and Grace*. 1954. Reprint, Chicago: Moody Press, 1967.

McGarvey, J.W. and Philip Y. Pendleton. *The Fourfold Gospel and Commentary on Acts of Apostles*. Tempe, AZ: The Crosswire Software and Bible Society, 1863, 1882.

McLean, John A. The Importance of Hermeneutics. In *The Fundamentals for the Twenty-first Century*, Mal Couch, ed. Grand Rapids, MI: Kregel Publications, 2000.

Mickelsen, A. Berkeley. *Romans* in *The Wycliffe Bible Commentary*, ed. Charles F. Pfeiffer and Everett F. Harrison. Nashville: The Southwestern Co, 1962.

Mindek, Douglas M. The Law and Evangelism. *Alliance Life*, June 6, 1990, 21.

Moo, Douglas J. *The Law of Christ as the Fulfillment of the Law of Moses: A Modified Lutheran View.* in Gundry, Stanley N. ed. *Five Views of Law and the Gospel*, Grand Rapids: Zondervan, 1996.

Moule, H.C.G. *Studies in Colossians & Philemon.* 1893. Reprint, Grand Rapids, MI, Kregel, 1983.

Newell, William R. *Hebrews: Verse by Verse.* Chicago: Moody Press, 1947.

Purkiser, W. T., Demaray, C.E., Metz, Donald S., Stuneck, Maude A. *Exploring the Old Testament*, Kansas City, MO: Beacon Hill Press of Kansas City, 1955.

Reagan, David R. Does the Law of Moses Apply to Christians? *Word and Work.* March 1995, 69–75.

Richardson, Alan. *A Theological Wordbook of the Bible.* New York: The MacMillan Company, 1950.

Ritchie, Rick. What is This Law and Gospel Thing? *Modern Reformation*, March/April 1993, 7–11.

Schofield, J.I. *Scofield Reference Notes*, on Matthew 21:43. 1917 Edition, Tempe, AZ: The Crosswire Software and Bible Society, 1810/1825.

Scot, D. Russell. Deuteronomy in *The Abingdon Bible Commentary.* Frederick C. Eiselen, Edwin Lewis, and David G. Downey ed. New York, Abingdon-Cokesbury Press, 1929.

Spence, H. D. M. St. Luke in the Pulpit Commentary, ed. H.D.M. Spence & Joseph Exell. New York: Funk & Wagnalls, 1913.

Stevens, George B. Gospel and Law in the Teaching of Jesus Christ. *Searching Together*, Spring-Autumn 1992, 9–16.

Strickland, Wayne G. The Inauguration of the Law of Christ with the Gospel of Christ: A Dispensational View. in Gundry, Stanley N. ed. *Five Views of Law and the Gospel*, Grand Rapids: Zondervan, 1996.

Strickland, Wayne G. The Inauguration of the Law of Christ with the Gospel of Christ: A Dispensational View. in Gundry, Stanley N. ed. *Five Views of Law and the Gospel*, (Grand Rapids: Zondervan, 1996).

Ungar, Merrill F. *Unger's Bible Handbook*. Chicago: Moody Press, 1966.

VanGemeren, William A. The Law is the Perfection of Righteousness in Jesus Christ: A Reformed Perspective. in Gundry, Stanley N. ed. *Five Views of Law and the Gospel*, Grand Rapids: Zondervan, 1996.

_____Response to The Inauguration of the Law of Christ with the Gospel of Christ: A Dispensational View, by Wayne Strickland in Gundry, Stanley N. ed. *Five Views of Law and the Gospel*, (Grand Rapids: Zondervan, 1996

_____Response to *The Theonomic Reformed Approach to Law and Gospel*. By Greg L. Bahnsen in Gundry, Stanley N. ed. *Five Views of Law and the Gospel*, Grand Rapids: Zondervan, 1996.

Vaughn, Harold. An Unscriptural Division. *The Baptist Examiner*. June 11, 1998, 1, 8, 9.

Vine, William. E. *An Expository Dictionary of Old Testament Words*. Edited by F. F. Bruce. Old Tappan, NJ: Fleming H. Revell Co., 1978.

Walther, C. F. W. *The Proper Distinction Between Law and Gospel*. (St. Louis, Concordia Publishing House, 1986), 1.

Wesley, John. *John Wesley's Notes on the Bible* Based on the electronic edition by Sulu Kelley and Bill Brown, Tempe, AZ, The Crosswire Software and Bible Society.

Ware, Bruce. *Baptism: Three Views.* David F. Wright, ed. Downers Grove, IL: IVP Academic, 2009.

Williams, A. Lukeyn. Matthew, vol. 1 in The *Pulpit Commentary,* ed. H.D.M. Spence & Joseph Exell. New York: Funk & Wagnalls, 1913.

Wuest, Kenneth S. *Galatians in Wuest's Word Studies in the Greek New Testament For the English Reader, Vol 1.* Grand Rapids, MI: William B. Eerdmans Publishing Company, 1944, reprint 1978.

_____Romans in *Wuest's Word Studies From the Greek New Testament For the English Reader, Vol 1.* Grand Rapids, MI: William B. Eerdmans Publishing Company, 1953, reprint 1978.

Young, D. Jeremiah, vol. 11 in *The Pulpit Commentary,* ed. H.D.M. Spence & Joseph Exell. New York: Funk & Wagnalls, 1913.

SCRIPTURE INDEX

For more information about
Lester Stephenson
&
A Biblicist View of Law and Gospel

please visit:

www.lstephensonwriter.com

For more information about
AMBASSADOR INTERNATIONAL
please visit:

www.ambassador-international.com
@AmbassadorIntl
www.facebook.com/AmbassadorIntl